Solopreneur

Andrew Parry

Published by Andrew Parry, 2024.

While every precaution has been taken in the preparation of this book, the publisher assumes no responsibility for errors or omissions, or for damages resulting from the use of the information contained herein.

SOLOPRENEUR

First edition. October 15, 2024.

ISBN: 979-8224849413

Written by Andrew Parry.

Table of Contents

The Rise of the Solopreneur in the Digital Age

In recent years, the term "solopreneur" has gained significant traction, and for good reason. As the digital age continues to expand, more individuals are choosing to run their businesses independently, with no need for employees, partners, or external management teams. Being a solopreneur is all about taking control of your business, being responsible for all aspects of it, and ultimately creating a life where you call the shots.

The digital revolution has been a key factor in making solopreneurship more accessible. Just a decade ago, starting and running a business meant large investments in office space, staff, and infrastructure. However, the rise of online platforms, digital tools, and social media has made it possible for individuals to launch, manage, and grow businesses entirely from a laptop, often with minimal upfront costs.

At the heart of this shift is the flexibility the digital age offers. Today's solopreneurs can sell physical or digital products, offer services, teach, coach, consult, or even become content creators. The digital space is vast and filled with opportunities, enabling solopreneurs to carve out niches that suit their skills and passions. You can be a graphic designer, freelance writer, digital marketer, or even a yoga instructor – whatever your skill set, the digital world allows you to reach a global audience with relative ease.

One of the most powerful aspects of being a solopreneur in the digital age is the autonomy it provides. Solopreneurs don't have to deal with office politics, hierarchy, or the complexities of managing a team. This independence allows them to focus entirely on their vision and their customers, creating highly personalized products and services. By being in control of every aspect of their business, solopreneurs can quickly adapt to market changes, make decisions swiftly, and maintain a hands-on approach in every facet of their venture.

However, with this independence comes the need for versatility. A solopreneur must wear many hats—marketer, accountant, customer service rep, strategist, and more. Fortunately, the same digital tools that make solopreneurship possible also make it easier to manage all these responsibilities. Cloud-based platforms like Google Workspace, project management tools like Asana, accounting software like QuickBooks, and marketing automation tools like Mailchimp allow solopreneurs to streamline their operations.

The rise of the gig economy has also contributed to the growth of solopreneurs. Freelance platforms such as Upwork, Fiverr, and Freelancer enable people to offer their skills and services to clients around the world, without the constraints of traditional employment. For many, freelancing is the gateway into solopreneurship, as it allows individuals to test the waters and build a client base before fully transitioning into running their own business.

Social media, too, plays a crucial role in the solopreneur's toolkit. Platforms like Instagram, Facebook, and LinkedIn are not just for socializing anymore; they are powerful business tools that enable solopreneurs to build brands, engage with audiences, and market products or services—all for free or at a low cost. Solopreneurs can now connect with their audience directly, build a loyal following, and create personalized content that resonates with their target market.

One of the most notable changes that the digital age has brought to solopreneurship is the removal of geographical barriers. In the past, small business owners were limited to their local markets. Now, with the internet, solopreneurs can offer products and services globally. E-commerce platforms like Shopify, Etsy, and Amazon make it possible to sell physical products to customers worldwide, while digital products, like e-books, online courses, and software, can be distributed instantly to anyone with an internet connection.

The rise of solopreneurship is also closely linked to changing attitudes about work-life balance. More people are seeking greater control over their time, opting to escape the traditional 9-to-5 workday in favor of a lifestyle that offers more freedom and flexibility. Solopreneurs can work from anywhere—whether it's a coffee shop, a home office, or a tropical beach. This flexibility allows for a more personalized work schedule, making it easier to prioritize family, health, and hobbies while still growing a successful business.

But with this freedom comes responsibility. Solopreneurs must be self-motivated and disciplined. Without a boss or team to hold them accountable, the success or failure of their business rests entirely on their shoulders. This requires a unique blend of creativity, resilience, and the ability to manage time effectively.

Another key factor driving the rise of solopreneurs is the increasing availability of education and resources. Today, anyone with an internet connection can learn virtually anything. From free YouTube tutorials to paid online courses on platforms like Udemy or Coursera, solopreneurs have access to a wealth of knowledge that can help them start and grow their businesses. This democratization of education has empowered people to gain the skills they need, whether that's learning how to code, mastering digital marketing, or understanding the fundamentals of business finance.

Furthermore, the rise of remote work due to the COVID-19 pandemic has accelerated the solopreneur trend. With many people forced to work from home, the line between traditional employment and solopreneurship began to blur. As companies adapted to remote work, individuals saw that they could be just as productive, if not more so, while working independently. For many, this realization became the catalyst to break away from the corporate world and pursue solopreneurship full-time.

The digital age has made solopreneurship not only feasible but also increasingly popular. It offers a level of autonomy, flexibility, and opportunity that was once unimaginable for solo business owners. As more people seek independence from traditional work structures, the solopreneur movement will continue to grow, reshaping the future of entrepreneurship.

In this new era, being a solopreneur means more than just running a business. It's about embracing the digital tools and platforms that allow you to connect with a global audience, streamline operations, and maintain the freedom to shape your work—and your life—on your own terms. The rise of solopreneurship is a testament to how technology, social media, and the internet have empowered individuals to take charge of their futures, making it possible for anyone with a dream and a laptop to build a business in the digital age.

Understanding What It Means to Be a Solopreneur

Being a solopreneur is about more than simply owning and running a business by yourself—it's about embodying a mindset that embraces independence, creativity, and self-reliance. A solopreneur isn't just an entrepreneur; they're someone who builds a business around their own skills, passions, and interests, taking full control of every aspect of their venture without the need for a team. In many ways, solopreneurship is an empowering path that offers both freedom and responsibility, allowing you to create a business that aligns with your personal vision and lifestyle.

At its core, a solopreneur operates alone. Unlike traditional entrepreneurs who may work with partners, investors, or hire staff to delegate tasks, a solopreneur takes on the role of business owner, manager, marketer, salesperson, and sometimes even customer service rep. This hands-on approach gives solopreneurs a deep connection to every aspect of their business, but it also requires a broad skill set and a willingness to constantly learn and adapt.

The allure of solopreneurship is often tied to the desire for freedom. Many people are drawn to this path because they want more control over their time, their work environment, and their life in general. As a solopreneur, you can set your own schedule, work from wherever you choose, and make decisions without needing approval from anyone else. Whether you're selling products, offering services, or running a digital business, solopreneurship offers the flexibility to structure your workday in a way that suits your needs.

But this freedom also comes with challenges. Since solopreneurs work independently, they are responsible for every facet of their business. That means managing the workload of multiple departments—marketing, finance, operations, and customer support—all on their own. This requires a level of discipline and time management that goes beyond a typical 9-to-5 job. There are no colleagues or managers to hold you accountable, so staying motivated and productive is a key part of solopreneur success.

One of the misconceptions about solopreneurs is that they have to do everything by themselves, all the time. While solopreneurs typically don't have full-time employees, many use freelancers, contractors, or automated systems to help with certain aspects of their business. For example, a solopreneur running an e-commerce business might hire a freelance web designer to build their site, use automation tools to handle marketing emails, and rely on virtual assistants for customer support. The key difference is that the solopreneur remains the sole decision-maker, responsible for the overall direction and strategy of the business.

Solopreneurship also requires a level of self-awareness. Since the business revolves around your skills and abilities, it's important to have a clear understanding of your strengths and weaknesses. Being honest with yourself about what you excel at—and what you may need to outsource or learn more about—is essential for long-term success. If you're great at creating products but struggle with marketing, for example, recognizing that early on can help you avoid potential pitfalls and ensure you're investing time in the right areas.

Another significant aspect of solopreneurship is the alignment between personal values and business goals. Unlike large corporations or traditional businesses, where the bottom line often takes precedence, solopreneurs can shape their business to reflect their values, passions, and long-term vision. This means that the work you do as a solopreneur is often deeply connected to your sense of purpose. Whether you're driven by creativity, a desire to help others, or the pursuit of financial independence, solopreneurship allows you to build a business that's a true extension of who you are.

In the digital age, solopreneurs have an abundance of tools and resources at their fingertips that make it easier to manage every aspect of their business. With the right digital tools, you can handle everything from invoicing to social media marketing with just a few clicks. This technological shift has made solopreneurship more accessible than ever before, allowing individuals to reach global audiences, automate routine tasks, and grow their business without the need for significant upfront capital.

However, solopreneurship also requires a high degree of adaptability. The business landscape, especially online, is constantly changing. New technologies emerge, market trends shift, and customer expectations evolve. As a solopreneur, you must be willing to stay informed and pivot your business when necessary. This might mean learning new skills, adopting new platforms, or changing your marketing strategy to stay competitive. The ability to evolve with the market is a crucial trait of successful solopreneurs.

Another critical aspect of solopreneurship is the relationship with customers or clients. Since you're the face of the business, building strong, personal relationships with your audience is essential. Solopreneurs often have closer, more direct interactions with their customers compared to larger companies. This can be a huge advantage, as it allows you to tailor your products, services, and communication to meet the specific needs and preferences of your audience. In many cases, this personal touch is what sets solopreneurs apart from larger competitors and fosters loyalty among customers.

Balancing personal and professional life can be a challenge for solopreneurs. Since you're working for yourself, it's easy to let the lines between work and home life blur. Many solopreneurs struggle with overworking, particularly in the early stages of their business when there's a lot to be done and not enough hours in the day. On the flip side, the freedom to set your own schedule means you can design your workday in a way that allows for a healthier work-life balance. It takes discipline to create boundaries between your business and personal life, but doing so is key to avoiding burnout.

Ultimately, solopreneurship is about taking full ownership of your professional journey. It's about leveraging your unique skills, ideas, and vision to create a business that aligns with your life goals. While it can be demanding, requiring you to juggle multiple roles and responsibilities, the rewards are immense. Solopreneurship offers the freedom to make your own decisions, the flexibility to design your own schedule, and the satisfaction of building something entirely on your own.

AS YOU CONTINUE ON your solopreneur journey, it's important to remember that success doesn't happen overnight. Building a business from the ground up takes time, effort, and a willingness to learn from mistakes along the way. However, the sense of accomplishment that comes from running a successful solopreneur venture is unparalleled. You'll not only have the satisfaction of knowing you did it all yourself, but you'll also gain invaluable skills and experiences that will serve you throughout your life.

Solopreneurship is more than just a career choice—it's a way of life. It's about taking control of your future, crafting a business around your passions, and having the confidence to go after your dreams on your own terms. And while the journey may be challenging, the potential for personal and professional growth makes it one of the most rewarding paths you can take.

Building the Mindset for Solopreneurship

The journey to becoming a solopreneur isn't just about acquiring the right skills or setting up the perfect business plan—it begins with cultivating the right mindset. Solopreneurship requires a unique way of thinking that blends resilience, self-motivation, adaptability, and an unwavering belief in yourself. Building this mindset is one of the most critical aspects of solopreneur success, because it serves as the foundation upon which your entire business is built.

At the heart of the solopreneur mindset is the concept of independence. As a solopreneur, you are responsible for every decision, every challenge, and every success that comes your way. Unlike a traditional job where you have supervisors, teams, or coworkers to lean on, solopreneurs rely on their own resourcefulness and problem-solving abilities. This independence is empowering, but it can also be intimidating, especially when things don't go as planned. That's why the first step in building the solopreneur mindset is embracing self-reliance and trusting in your ability to navigate obstacles on your own.

Self-discipline is another critical component. Without a boss setting deadlines or a team to hold you accountable, you must be able to manage your time and stay focused. Solopreneurship offers incredible freedom, but that freedom can easily turn into procrastination if you aren't careful. Building the discipline to consistently work on your business—whether you feel like it or not—is what separates successful solopreneurs from those who struggle to gain traction. This doesn't mean working nonstop, but rather developing a routine that balances productivity with flexibility.

Another key part of the solopreneur mindset is resilience. As a solopreneur, you will face setbacks. There will be days when you doubt your choices, when sales are slow, or when a project doesn't turn out the way you envisioned. The ability to bounce back from these moments of frustration is essential. Solopreneurs need to have thick skin and a refusal to give up when things get tough. Instead of viewing failures as the end of the road, solopreneurs see them as opportunities to learn and grow. This resilience isn't just about enduring tough times; it's about thriving in them by staying focused on the bigger picture.

One of the most important shifts in mindset for solopreneurs is transitioning from an employee mentality to an entrepreneurial one. When you work for someone else, you're usually focused on completing tasks that are assigned to you. As a solopreneur, your focus shifts from tasks to results. It's no longer about what you're doing day-to-day but rather about the overall impact you're creating in your business. This mindset shift is crucial because it forces you to think strategically rather than simply reactively. You begin to ask yourself, "How does this action move my business forward?" instead of "What do I need to get done today?"

A solopreneur's mindset also includes an openness to continual learning. The digital landscape is always evolving, and new tools, platforms, and strategies emerge regularly. Solopreneurs who are successful in the long run have a passion for learning and a willingness to adapt. This could mean learning new marketing techniques, staying up-to-date with changes in your industry, or even mastering new technologies that make running your business more efficient. The mindset of a lifelong learner ensures that you remain relevant and competitive in your field.

In addition to being adaptable, solopreneurs must also be visionary. As the sole architect of your business, you need to be able to see the bigger picture. This means setting clear goals for where you want your business to go and having the foresight to anticipate potential challenges or opportunities. Vision isn't just about dreaming big; it's about being able to break those dreams down into actionable steps. Solopreneurs with a clear vision are able to stay focused on their long-term goals, even when the day-to-day tasks seem overwhelming.

Self-confidence is another critical piece of the solopreneur mindset puzzle. You are your business, and if you don't believe in yourself, it will be hard to convince customers, clients, or partners to believe in you either. Building self-confidence doesn't happen overnight, but it can be cultivated by setting small goals and achieving them. As you rack up these wins, your belief in your ability to succeed grows. Confidence also means trusting your instincts and being comfortable making decisions without second-guessing yourself at every turn.

However, solopreneurship isn't just about personal confidence—it's also about having a growth mindset. A growth mindset is the belief that abilities and intelligence can be developed through effort, learning, and perseverance. Solopreneurs with a growth mindset are not afraid of challenges; they embrace them because they know that each challenge is an opportunity to expand their skills and grow their business. When something goes wrong, solopreneurs with a growth mindset don't think, "I'm a failure." Instead, they ask, "What can I learn from this?"

Another essential part of the solopreneur mindset is the ability to manage fear. Fear of failure, fear of the unknown, and even fear of success can be paralyzing for anyone trying to build a business. Successful solopreneurs acknowledge these fears but don't let them dictate their actions. Instead, they use fear as a motivator to take calculated risks, push out of their comfort zones, and strive for greatness. The ability to act despite fear is a hallmark of entrepreneurial thinking.

Additionally, solopreneurs need to develop a strong sense of purpose. Purpose is what drives you to get up in the morning and work on your business, even when it's challenging. It's the reason behind why you're doing what you're doing. For some solopreneurs, purpose might be tied to financial freedom, creative expression, or helping others. Whatever your purpose is, keeping it front and center will help you stay motivated and focused, especially during the more difficult moments of your journey.

Lastly, the solopreneur mindset includes understanding the importance of balance. Being your own boss is exhilarating, but it can also lead to burnout if you don't manage your energy and time effectively. Solopreneurs often wear many hats, and it's easy to fall into the trap of working around the clock. While hard work is a key component of success, maintaining your physical and mental well-being is equally important. Successful solopreneurs know when to push themselves and when to step back and recharge.

In essence, building the solopreneur mindset is about fostering independence, resilience, adaptability, and a hunger for growth. It's about shifting from a task-focused employee mindset to a results-driven entrepreneurial one. It's about believing in yourself and your vision while being open to learning and growing along the way. Developing this mindset isn't just crucial for success—it's what makes the solopreneur journey rewarding in itself.

Why Solopreneurs Thrive in Today's Economy

Solopreneurs are thriving in today's economy because the landscape of business has fundamentally shifted. The rise of technology, the evolution of consumer behavior, and the increasing desire for autonomy and flexibility have all converged to create an ideal environment for those who want to run a business on their own terms. Today, more than ever, solopreneurs have access to the tools, platforms, and resources needed to not only survive but to flourish in a world that values independence, innovation, and personal branding.

One of the biggest reasons solopreneurs are thriving is the rapid advancement of technology. The digital age has opened up unprecedented opportunities for individuals to start and run businesses from virtually anywhere. Whether it's creating digital products, offering freelance services, or launching an e-commerce store, technology has leveled the playing field. Cloud-based platforms, automation tools, and online marketplaces allow solopreneurs to handle tasks that previously required entire teams. For example, tools like Shopify enable solopreneurs to build and manage an online store with minimal technical knowledge, while platforms like Upwork and Fiverr make it easy to find clients globally. This means that solopreneurs no longer need the infrastructure of a traditional business; they can run their operations with just a laptop and an internet connection.

The shift towards a gig economy has also played a pivotal role in the success of solopreneurs. More people are turning away from traditional employment in favor of freelance work, contract jobs, or project-based opportunities. This has normalized the concept of independent work and opened up new avenues for solopreneurs to find clients and projects.

Platforms such as Uber, Airbnb, and Etsy have further cemented the idea that individuals can monetize their skills, assets, or products without the need for a full-time job or a large company backing them. As a result, solopreneurs are able to thrive by tapping into these flexible work models, catering to a growing market of clients and consumers who value specialized, independent services.

Another factor contributing to the success of solopreneurs is the rise of personal branding. In today's economy, consumers are more interested in authentic, personalized experiences. Solopreneurs have the advantage of being able to offer this in a way that larger companies often cannot. By building a personal brand around their business, solopreneurs can establish deeper connections with their audience, create trust, and stand out in crowded markets. Social media platforms like Instagram, YouTube, and LinkedIn allow solopreneurs to showcase their personality, share their expertise, and engage directly with their customers. This direct line of communication helps solopreneurs create a sense of loyalty and community around their brand, which is increasingly important in a world where consumers crave genuine connections.

IN ADDITION TO TECHNOLOGY and personal branding, the low barriers to entry are another reason solopreneurs are thriving. Starting a business today no longer requires a large upfront investment or extensive resources. Thanks to online platforms, anyone can launch a business with relatively little capital. For instance, digital products such as e-books, online courses, or print-on-demand merchandise allow solopreneurs to create and sell products with minimal risk. Crowdfunding platforms like Kickstarter or Patreon provide additional avenues for raising capital without traditional loans or investors. This ease of entry encourages more people to pursue their passions and turn them into viable businesses, driving the solopreneur movement forward.

The changing nature of consumer behavior also plays a key role in solopreneur success. Consumers are becoming more discerning and selective about where they spend their money, and many are turning to small, independent businesses for unique, personalized products and services. The modern consumer values authenticity, sustainability, and the stories behind the brands they support. Solopreneurs, who often infuse their personal values and stories into their businesses, are well-positioned to meet this demand. Whether it's a handmade product, a niche digital service, or a specialized consultation, solopreneurs can offer something that feels more intimate and tailored than what larger corporations can provide.

In addition, solopreneurs benefit from the rise of niche markets. The internet has made it easier for individuals to find and serve specific audiences with very particular needs or interests. Solopreneurs can tap into these niches in ways that large companies often overlook or find unprofitable. By focusing on a targeted group of consumers, solopreneurs can build dedicated, loyal followings. Whether it's offering eco-friendly products, specialized coaching services, or crafting content for a particular subculture, solopreneurs can cater to unique demands and establish themselves as experts in their chosen niches.

The flexibility and agility of solopreneurs are additional reasons why they thrive in today's economy. Larger companies often have rigid structures and slower decision-making processes, which can make them less responsive to market changes. Solopreneurs, on the other hand, can pivot quickly and adapt to new trends, consumer behaviors, or industry shifts.

This nimbleness allows solopreneurs to take advantage of new opportunities and stay ahead of competitors who are slower to react. Whether it's adopting a new social media platform, launching a trending product, or adjusting pricing strategies, solopreneurs can make changes almost instantaneously.

Furthermore, the desire for work-life balance has driven many to the solopreneur path. Traditional corporate jobs often come with long hours, rigid schedules, and little flexibility. Solopreneurs have the freedom to design their workdays in ways that suit their personal lives. This appeal of autonomy and flexibility has attracted people from all walks of life—whether it's parents seeking more time with their children, digital nomads looking to travel the world while working, or individuals simply wanting more control over their time. As more people prioritize a balanced lifestyle, solopreneurship becomes an increasingly attractive option.

Solopreneurs are also uniquely positioned to take advantage of the power of automation. In today's economy, there are countless tools available to streamline business processes, from customer relationship management (CRM) systems to email marketing platforms and payment processors. Solopreneurs can automate much of their day-to-day operations, allowing them to focus on creative or strategic aspects of their business. This efficiency not only saves time but also allows solopreneurs to scale their businesses without the need to hire additional staff.

Lastly, the societal shift towards valuing entrepreneurship has contributed to the thriving solopreneur landscape. Today, entrepreneurship is often celebrated, and being your own boss is seen as a desirable career path. More people are seeking independence and are willing to take risks in pursuit of their dreams. As this cultural shift continues, solopreneurs are finding more support, resources, and communities that encourage independent business ownership. From coworking spaces to online courses designed specifically for solopreneurs, the ecosystem around entrepreneurship has grown, providing a wealth of opportunities for those willing to step out on their own.

In conclusion, solopreneurs are thriving in today's economy because they are perfectly aligned with the values and trends of the modern world. Technology, personal branding, low barriers to entry, and the demand for authenticity have all created fertile ground for solopreneurs to succeed. As the economy continues to evolve, solopreneurs are likely to play an increasingly prominent role, reshaping how we think about work, business, and success in the 21st century.

How to Identify Your Passion and Turn It into a Business

Identifying your passion and turning it into a business is a dream for many, but the path to making that dream a reality requires introspection, planning, and strategy. At its core, building a business around your passion means aligning your personal interests, strengths, and values with a product or service that can solve a problem or fulfill a need in the market. This alignment not only makes your business more sustainable but also ensures that you remain motivated and fulfilled while running it.

The first step to identifying your passion is simple: ask yourself what you genuinely enjoy doing. What are the activities or topics that excite you, that you can lose yourself in for hours without even noticing? Your passion might be a hobby, a skill you've honed over the years, or something you've always been interested in but never pursued fully. Think about what energizes you and sparks your curiosity. For some, their passion is clear—they love painting, writing, cooking, or playing music. For others, identifying passion requires more digging. If you're unsure, start by reflecting on the following questions:

What are your favorite hobbies or activities when you're not working?

What subjects do you love to read about or research?

What do people often ask you for help with or advice on?

What are the skills you're naturally good at?

What types of problems do you enjoy solving?

Answering these questions can help you zero in on your passion. Once you have a sense of what truly excites you, the next step is to determine if it has the potential to be turned into a business. This is where aligning your passion with market demand becomes essential. Having a passion for something is fantastic, but if there's no market for it, it may not translate into a viable business. The key is to find the intersection between what you love to do and what people are willing to pay for.

To assess whether your passion can become a business, start by researching your potential market. Who are the people who would benefit from or enjoy what you offer? Is there a problem you can solve for them, or a gap in the market that your passion can fill? Look at similar businesses in your field. Are there other people making a living from your passion? If so, what are they doing well, and where are the opportunities to differentiate yourself? Competition in a market can be a positive sign—it shows that there's demand for what you want to offer. One effective way to explore market demand is to test your idea on a small scale. Before you invest significant time and money into launching a full business, consider offering your product or service in a more informal way to see how people respond. For example, if you're passionate about photography, start by offering photo sessions to friends or through platforms like Instagram. If your passion is writing, publish blog posts, articles, or short stories online to gauge interest. Testing the waters allows you to gather feedback, refine your offerings, and ensure that there's a demand for what you're passionate about.

Once you've identified that there's a market for your passion, the next step is to determine how to monetize it. Ask yourself, "How can I take what I love and turn it into a product or service that people will pay for?" This might involve selling physical products, offering a service, teaching or coaching others, or creating digital products like e-books, courses, or memberships. The monetization strategy you choose will depend on the nature of your passion and the needs of your target audience.

If your passion is in a creative field like art, music, or writing, consider selling your creations, offering freelance services, or teaching your craft to others. Many solopreneurs find success by offering workshops, creating digital products, or launching subscription-based services. If your passion is fitness or wellness, for example, you might offer personal training sessions, start an online fitness community, or create instructional videos. The possibilities are endless, but the key is to tailor your monetization strategy to both your strengths and your audience's needs.

In many cases, turning your passion into a business will also require you to develop new skills or knowledge. For example, if you're passionate about baking and want to open a bakery, you may need to learn about food regulations, business management, and marketing. Don't let this intimidate you—view it as an opportunity to grow and expand your expertise. The beauty of solopreneurship is that you can evolve as your business evolves. The more you learn, the more equipped you'll be to turn your passion into a profitable venture.

A critical aspect of turning your passion into a business is ensuring that your enthusiasm doesn't fizzle out once it becomes work. Many solopreneurs struggle with the transition from doing something they love for fun to doing it for profit. To maintain your passion, focus on preserving the elements of your business that bring you joy. For example, if you love writing but find the administrative side of your business draining, consider outsourcing tasks like invoicing or social media management so that you can focus on your creative work. By delegating or automating less enjoyable tasks, you can keep your passion alive while running a sustainable business.

Another important consideration is to align your business with your personal values and long-term goals. Turning your passion into a business isn't just about making money; it's about building a life that reflects what matters most to you. Consider the lifestyle you want to create. Do you value flexibility and want the freedom to work from anywhere? Do you want to build a business that allows you to make a positive impact on others? By aligning your business with your values, you'll be more likely to stay motivated and fulfilled in the long run.

As you build your passion-driven business, remember that success doesn't happen overnight. It takes time, effort, and persistence to turn a passion into a profitable venture. Be patient with yourself, and don't be discouraged by setbacks. The road to solopreneurship is filled with challenges, but it's also incredibly rewarding. Every small step you take brings you closer to the life you've envisioned, and the satisfaction of building a business around something you love is unparalleled.

One of the most fulfilling aspects of turning your passion into a business is the personal growth that comes with it. As you navigate the ups and downs of entrepreneurship, you'll learn more about yourself, your strengths, and your ability to persevere. This journey of self-discovery is often one of the greatest rewards of solopreneurship. You're not just building a business—you're building a life that's aligned with your passions, values, and vision for the future.

In conclusion, identifying your passion and turning it into a business is a deeply personal and rewarding journey. By reflecting on what excites you, aligning it with market demand, and developing a strategy to monetize your passion, you can create a business that not only supports you financially but also fuels your sense of purpose and fulfillment. The key is to stay patient, be adaptable, and remain true to yourself as you navigate the path of solopreneurship.

Finding Ideas for Non-Digital Products That Stand Out

Finding ideas for non-digital products that stand out in today's competitive market can seem challenging, but with a little creativity and insight into consumer behavior, it's entirely possible to carve out a niche and offer something unique. The key to developing a successful non-digital product lies in identifying a tangible need, leveraging your own skills or interests, and creating something that resonates with your target audience. Whether you're drawn to handmade crafts, custom physical goods, or innovative practical solutions, there are plenty of ways to stand out by offering a product that customers want and can't find elsewhere.

The first step in discovering a great idea for a non-digital product is observation. Pay attention to the products that you use daily, and think about what could be improved or what's missing in the market. For instance, is there a tool or product you wish existed to make your daily tasks easier? Often, the best ideas come from solving a problem that you or someone you know has encountered. Many successful product ideas arise from personal experiences, where a creator saw a gap in the market and decided to fill it.

One of the most effective ways to brainstorm ideas for non-digital products is to focus on a specific niche. Instead of trying to create something that appeals to a broad audience, think about particular groups of people who have specialized needs or interests. Niche markets, though smaller, often have highly dedicated customers who are willing to pay for unique or high-quality items. For example, niche hobbies like woodworking, gardening, or even pet care offer plenty of opportunities to create products that cater to passionate enthusiasts. When you serve a niche market, you can develop products that truly stand out because they are designed with a specific audience in mind.

Another approach to finding non-digital product ideas is to tap into trends and societal shifts. Consider the growing demand for eco-friendly, sustainable products. As more consumers become environmentally conscious, they are looking for alternatives to single-use plastics, fast fashion, and disposable goods.

This trend has opened up a wealth of opportunities for solopreneurs who want to create products that align with these values. You could create reusable household items, ethically sourced clothing, or biodegradable packaging solutions. By offering products that contribute to a more sustainable lifestyle, you not only differentiate yourself but also tap into a rapidly growing market.

Handcrafted and artisanal products are also in high demand, as consumers increasingly seek out one-of-a-kind items that are made with care and attention to detail. If you have a craft or trade skill—such as woodworking, knitting, ceramics, or jewelry-making—you can create unique, handmade items that stand out in a world of mass-produced goods. What sets handmade products apart is the personal touch and craftsmanship involved, something that resonates deeply with buyers looking for authenticity and uniqueness. Platforms like Etsy have made it easier than ever to connect with buyers who value handmade, artisanal goods.

If you're looking for inspiration, think about ways to improve or add value to existing products. Take a common product and find ways to enhance it. This could mean making it more durable, more versatile, or more aesthetically pleasing. For example, a simple kitchen utensil could be redesigned with better ergonomics, or a backpack could be enhanced with more compartments and water-resistant material. Many successful solopreneurs have found success by taking everyday items and giving them a creative twist that solves a common problem or improves functionality.

Personalization is another powerful way to stand out in the world of non-digital products. People love products that feel like they were made just for them. Offering customization options—whether it's personalized engravings, custom color schemes, or made-to-order designs—can make your products more appealing to buyers who want something unique. Personalized gifts, in particular, are highly sought after for occasions like weddings, birthdays, and anniversaries. If you can offer a product that people can tailor to their preferences, you're giving them an opportunity to purchase something that feels special and distinct.

Finding inspiration for non-digital products can also come from examining the intersection of traditional crafts and modern needs. In today's fast-paced world, there's a growing appreciation for products that bring a sense of nostalgia or tradition, yet serve practical purposes for modern consumers. For example, handmade leather goods, vintage-inspired home décor, or artisanal stationery can all appeal to buyers who value craftsmanship but also want items they can use in their daily lives. By combining traditional techniques with contemporary design, you can create products that stand out as both functional and stylish.

Another area of opportunity lies in solving pain points that consumers face in their daily lives. Think about the inconveniences or frustrations people experience and how you can create a product that alleviates those issues. For example, if people often complain about disorganized workspaces, you could create a line of desk organizers or storage solutions that help keep things tidy and functional. Products that solve practical problems are highly valued, and if you can address a common pain point with an innovative solution, you'll have a strong foundation for a standout product.

Don't overlook the power of packaging and presentation in making your product stand out. Even the simplest of products can gain a premium feel through thoughtful packaging. Consider eco-friendly or minimalist designs that align with the values of your target audience. Attractive, sustainable, or clever packaging can elevate a product and make it more memorable to consumers. In some cases, the unboxing experience itself becomes part of the product's appeal, especially when you add personalized touches like handwritten notes or beautifully designed wrapping.

Local sourcing and supporting small-scale suppliers can also make your product more appealing, particularly to consumers who value ethical consumption. If your product is made with locally sourced materials, environmentally friendly practices, or supports artisans and small communities, make sure to highlight this in your marketing. Consumers increasingly want to know the story behind the products they buy, and if you can tell a compelling story about how your product is made, it can give you a competitive edge.

Lastly, one of the most straightforward ways to find non-digital product ideas is to simply ask your audience. If you already have a following on social media or a customer base, engage with them to find out what they want or need. Use surveys, polls, or direct conversations to get feedback on what types of products they would be excited about. By involving your audience in the product development process, you not only ensure that there's demand for what you're creating but also strengthen your relationship with your customers.

In conclusion, finding ideas for non-digital products that stand out requires a blend of creativity, market awareness, and an understanding of consumer needs. Whether you focus on niche markets, sustainability, handcrafted items, or solving practical problems, the key is to offer something that resonates with your audience and adds value to their lives. By aligning your product ideas with current trends, offering personalization, or tapping into traditional craftsmanship, you can create products that are not only unique but also compelling to consumers in today's market.

How to Brainstorm Digital Product Ideas That Sell

Brainstorming digital product ideas that sell is both an exciting and strategic process. In today's digital age, there's a seemingly endless range of possibilities for creating valuable, profitable digital products, but to succeed, you need to come up with ideas that not only inspire you but also meet the demands of your target audience. Whether you're interested in creating online courses, e-books, software, or memberships, the key is to identify opportunities where you can leverage your expertise, skills, and creativity to offer something that people are willing to pay for.

The first step in brainstorming digital product ideas is to focus on your own strengths and passions. Start by asking yourself what you're good at and what knowledge you have that others might find valuable. Do you have expertise in a particular field? Are you skilled at teaching or explaining complex topics in simple terms? Can you create content that entertains or inspires others? By identifying your unique strengths, you can begin to focus on digital products that allow you to share that expertise in a way that others will find helpful or engaging.

One effective way to spark ideas for digital products is to think about problems you've solved for yourself or others. What challenges have you faced, and how did you overcome them? Chances are, if you've encountered a specific problem, others have too. For example, if you've mastered the art of time management after years of struggling with procrastination, you could create an online course or e-book on productivity hacks. If you've developed a way to streamline social media marketing for small businesses, you could create a set of digital templates or a guide that helps others do the same. Solving a specific problem through a digital product not only adds value to your audience but also positions you as an expert in that area.

It's also helpful to look at trends and emerging markets when brainstorming digital product ideas. Stay informed about what's popular and what's gaining traction in your industry or niche. Are people increasingly interested in learning about a particular topic? Is there a growing demand for certain types of digital products, such as online courses or software tools? By paying attention to what's trending, you can identify opportunities to create products that are timely and relevant. However, it's important not to chase trends for the sake of it—make sure your digital product ideas still align with your expertise and passion.

Another powerful brainstorming technique is to look at what others in your industry are doing successfully. Take some time to research competitors or leaders in your niche who are already selling digital products. What types of products are they offering? What seems to be working well for them? This research can help you identify gaps in the market where you can innovate or offer a fresh perspective. For example, if you notice that there are several online courses on a specific topic but none of them are particularly in-depth, you could create a more comprehensive or specialized version that fills that gap.

When brainstorming, don't limit yourself to just one type of digital product. Consider the wide range of digital products that can be created today. Some popular options include:

E-books: If you're knowledgeable in a particular field or have a lot of experience to share, writing an e-book can be a great way to package that information into a digestible format. E-books are popular because they're easy to create, distribute, and update as needed.

Online courses: People are always looking to improve themselves, whether it's learning a new skill or gaining deeper knowledge in a specific area. If you're skilled in teaching, creating an online course can be a highly profitable digital product. Platforms like Teachable and Udemy make it simple to host and sell your courses to a global audience.

Templates and tools: Digital templates, such as design assets, marketing calendars, or budgeting spreadsheets, are in high demand because they save people time and effort. If you can create a tool that helps your target audience streamline their work or personal lives, you have a potential winning product.

Membership sites: If your digital product idea involves ongoing value or content, consider creating a membership site. This could involve providing exclusive access to tutorials, resources, or community support. Membership sites work well because they provide recurring income, and loyal customers often appreciate the ongoing value they receive.

Digital art and design: For creatives, selling digital art, illustrations, or design elements can be a lucrative business. Whether it's selling stock photos, custom graphics, or downloadable artwork, there's a growing market for digital creatives who want to monetize their talents.

Software and apps: If you have technical skills, developing software or apps that solve a specific problem or meet a particular need can be a highly profitable digital product. Whether it's a productivity tool, a creative app, or a business solution, digital products in the form of software are in high demand.

Once you have a few ideas in mind, it's time to validate them. One of the most important steps in creating a successful digital product is ensuring there's demand for it before you invest too much time and effort into development. There are several ways you can validate your ideas:

Ask your audience: If you already have a following on social media, a blog, or an email list, ask your audience what they would find most valuable. You can create polls, surveys, or even engage in one-on-one conversations to get a sense of what people are looking for and would be willing to purchase.

Look at existing products: Research similar digital products in the market. Are they selling well? Check out reviews, testimonials, or case studies to see what customers love about these products and where they feel improvements could be made. This research can help you refine your idea and make your product even better than what's currently available.

Pre-sell your product: Before you fully create your digital product, consider offering it for pre-sale. This approach can be particularly useful for e-books, online courses, or memberships. By offering a discounted rate for early buyers, you can gauge interest and gather feedback before completing the final product. If people are willing to pay for your product before it's finished, that's a strong sign of demand.

Test a free version: Another way to validate your digital product idea is by offering a free version or a smaller sample of it to see how your audience responds. For example, if you're considering creating an online course, offer a free mini-course or an e-book on the same topic. If it attracts attention and engagement, you'll know that there's potential for a paid, full-scale version.

As you brainstorm, don't forget the importance of staying flexible and open to new ideas. The digital world is constantly evolving, and consumer needs shift over time. While it's important to plan and focus on your product's core offering, leaving room for experimentation and iteration can help you adapt to market changes and discover unexpected opportunities.

Finally, ensure that whatever digital product you create aligns with your long-term vision and brand. It's easy to get swept up in trends or popular ideas, but the most successful digital products are those that reflect your passion, expertise, and the unique value you bring to the table. By staying authentic to your brand and focusing on delivering real value to your audience, you'll be able to create digital products that not only sell but also help you build a loyal customer base.

In summary, brainstorming digital product ideas that sell requires a balance of self-reflection, market research, and creative thinking. By focusing on your strengths, identifying customer pain points, and staying attuned to trends, you can come up with ideas that not only resonate with your target audience but also allow you to create a sustainable and profitable solopreneur business.

Creating a Unique Value Proposition as a Solopreneur

Creating a unique value proposition (UVP) is one of the most crucial steps in building a successful solopreneur business. Your UVP is the clear statement that defines what makes your product or service different from—and better than—the competition. It's not just about what you offer, but why a customer should choose you over others. In a marketplace filled with countless products and services, having a strong UVP is essential for standing out and attracting customers who resonate with your brand. As a solopreneur, your unique value proposition is particularly important because you're often competing against larger companies with more resources. The good news is that solopreneurs have the flexibility and authenticity to craft a UVP that's deeply personal and tailored to the exact needs of their niche market. A well-crafted UVP serves as the backbone of your marketing and communication strategies, helping you connect with the right customers in a way that feels genuine and compelling.

The first step in creating your unique value proposition is understanding who your target audience is. You need to know what drives your potential customers, what their needs are, and what problems they're trying to solve. This requires in-depth research and often direct interaction with your audience. Understanding your customer's pain points allows you to position your product or service as the perfect solution. For example, if you're offering productivity tools for freelancers, you need to identify the specific frustrations they face, such as managing time effectively or juggling multiple projects. By deeply understanding these issues, you can shape your UVP around how your product makes their lives easier or more efficient.

Once you've identified your target audience and their needs, the next step is to clarify what makes your business different from others. This differentiation is key to your UVP. It could be the quality of your product, a unique feature, the way you deliver your service, or even the customer experience you offer. It might also be your personal story or the values your business stands for. As a solopreneur, you have the advantage of offering a personal touch that larger corporations often lack. Your customers might value the direct connection they get with you, or they might appreciate the craftsmanship and passion behind your work. Whatever it is, your UVP should highlight what sets you apart and why that matters to your audience.

In crafting your UVP, consider the following questions:

What problem does my product or service solve?

How does my solution improve the customer's life or business?

What are the benefits of choosing my product or service over the competition?

What unique skills, experience, or perspective do I bring to the table?

What are the emotional and practical benefits of working with me specifically?

Answering these questions will help you distill the essence of your business and focus on the core elements that make your offer compelling.

One important aspect of a strong UVP is that it speaks to the emotional and practical benefits of your product or service. It's not enough to say what you offer; you need to communicate how it makes your customer's life better or easier. For example, if you sell handmade leather goods, your UVP shouldn't just focus on the craftsmanship. It should also highlight how the product adds value to the customer's life—perhaps by providing a durable, stylish accessory that can last a lifetime and offer a sense of luxury and individuality.

A powerful UVP also addresses objections or concerns that potential customers might have. Consider what might hold someone back from purchasing your product or service. Is it price, quality, convenience, or something else? By addressing these concerns directly in your UVP, you can alleviate doubts and build trust. For instance, if you know that customers may hesitate due to the price of your product, you can emphasize the long-term value and durability that make it worth the investment.

Keep in mind that your UVP should be clear and concise. A complicated or vague UVP will confuse potential customers and dilute your message. The best UVPs are straightforward, focusing on one or two key aspects that make your business stand out. Instead of trying to appeal to everyone, focus on being crystal clear about the value you offer to your specific audience. A compelling UVP often boils down to a simple, memorable phrase or sentence that encapsulates the core benefit of your product or service.

To help you craft your UVP, consider this basic formula:

"I help [target audience] with [problem], by offering [unique solution], which results in [key benefit]."

For example, if you're a solopreneur offering social media management for small businesses, your UVP might be:

"I help small business owners grow their online presence by managing their social media accounts, freeing up their time and driving more engagement from their audience."

Once you have your UVP, it's important to incorporate it into every aspect of your business. It should be prominently displayed on your website, featured in your marketing materials, and used in your conversations with potential customers. Your UVP isn't just a one-time statement; it should be the foundation of how you communicate the value of your business consistently and authentically.

Incorporating your UVP into your branding is crucial. Your branding should reflect the promise of your UVP and align with the values and expectations of your target audience. From your website's design to the tone of your social media posts, everything should reinforce the message of your UVP. If your UVP is about providing a premium, luxurious experience, for example, your website should feel high-end, and your customer service should be impeccable. If your UVP emphasizes simplicity and efficiency, your processes, communication, and product delivery should mirror that promise.

As a solopreneur, your unique value proposition will likely evolve over time as your business grows and the market shifts. It's important to regularly revisit your UVP to ensure it's still relevant and effective. As you gain more insights into your customers and your market, you may discover new ways to differentiate yourself or highlight additional benefits that resonate with your audience.

To summarize, creating a unique value proposition as a solopreneur involves identifying your audience's needs, differentiating your business from the competition, and clearly communicating the benefits of your product or service. Your UVP is the cornerstone of your marketing efforts and helps you stand out in a crowded market. By focusing on what makes your offer special and why it matters to your customers, you'll be able to attract the right people and build a loyal customer base that appreciates the value you bring.

The Power of Niche Markets for Solopreneurs

Niche markets hold incredible power for solopreneurs, offering the opportunity to create a thriving business by serving a specific, focused audience. Unlike trying to compete in broad, overcrowded markets, solopreneurs who tap into a niche are able to build stronger connections with their customers, tailor their products or services to meet precise needs, and create a brand that stands out for its specialization. The beauty of niche markets is that they allow solopreneurs to build a sustainable business by being experts in a particular field, and the depth of that expertise is what sets them apart from the competition.

One of the key advantages of focusing on a niche market is the ability to target a specific group of people with unique needs. When you choose a niche, you're not trying to be everything to everyone. Instead, you're positioning yourself as the go-to expert for a particular type of product or service. This specificity allows you to focus your marketing, messaging, and product development on a clearly defined audience, which ultimately leads to better results. For example, rather than being a general health coach, you could narrow your focus to offering coaching for busy professionals looking to balance work and wellness. This allows you to speak directly to the pain points and challenges of that audience, offering them a solution that feels personalized and relevant.

Niche markets are particularly advantageous for solopreneurs because they allow you to compete effectively with larger businesses. Trying to appeal to a broad audience can quickly put a solopreneur at a disadvantage against bigger companies with more resources, larger teams, and significant advertising budgets. However, when you narrow your focus to a specific niche, you can carve out a space where you don't need to compete on size or scale. Instead, you can offer specialized expertise or a unique approach that larger businesses can't match. Your small size becomes an asset because it allows you to be more agile, flexible, and responsive to your customers' needs.

Another significant benefit of niche markets is customer loyalty. When you serve a niche, your customers are more likely to feel that you truly understand their specific needs and challenges. This deep connection fosters trust, and trust builds loyalty.

Solopreneurs who position themselves as experts within a niche often find that their customers return again and again because they feel confident that the products or services being offered are tailored precisely for them. Whether you're offering bespoke products, personalized services, or expert advice, a niche audience is more likely to appreciate and value what you provide.

Moreover, when you operate within a niche market, you're often able to charge premium prices. Customers who are looking for highly specialized solutions are usually willing to pay more for products or services that meet their exact requirements. This is because niche products often address very specific pain points that general solutions do not. For example, if you specialize in creating custom meal plans for athletes training for marathons, your expertise in that specific area makes your service more valuable to your audience compared to a generic nutritionist. In niche markets, value is perceived not just in the product or service itself, but in the fact that it has been designed with a deep understanding of the customer's unique needs.

Finding your niche begins with understanding your own strengths, passions, and experiences. What do you know deeply? What are you passionate about? What problems have you solved for yourself or others that others may struggle with? Often, the best niche ideas come from personal experience, where you've already identified a problem that you've successfully navigated. Think about the specific skills or knowledge that set you apart. This will often provide insight into the niche you're best suited to serve. In addition to understanding your strengths, it's important to consider where demand exists.

While it's essential to be passionate about your niche, you also need to ensure that there's a market for your product or service. This involves researching whether people are actively seeking solutions in your chosen area and if they're willing to pay for them. One way to assess demand is to look at online forums, social media groups, and other communities where people discuss their needs and frustrations related to your niche. Pay attention to the questions they ask and the problems they're trying to solve. This can give you insight into how you can position your offering as the perfect solution.

Once you've identified your niche, it's important to dive deep into understanding your target audience. The more specific and detailed you can get about who your customers are, the better you'll be able to serve them. This goes beyond demographics like age or location. Think about their behaviors, preferences, challenges, and motivations. What are their biggest pain points, and how can your product or service solve them? What are their goals, and how does what you offer help them achieve those goals? By getting to know your niche audience on a granular level, you can tailor your marketing, messaging, and product development to resonate deeply with them.

The power of niche markets for solopreneurs also lies in the fact that they allow you to create highly targeted marketing strategies. When you know exactly who you're speaking to, your marketing becomes more focused and effective. Rather than casting a wide net and hoping to catch a few interested customers, you can zero in on where your niche audience hangs out and what they care about. Whether it's through content marketing, social media, or direct outreach, your marketing efforts will be more impactful when they are designed to speak directly to the needs and desires of a specific group.

In niche markets, word-of-mouth and community support are also incredibly strong. When you provide specialized products or services that meet the needs of a tight-knit group, your customers are more likely to refer you to others in their community. Word-of-mouth marketing can be especially powerful in niche markets where customers are looking for trusted recommendations from people they know. By building a loyal customer base within a niche, solopreneurs can tap into a steady stream of referrals and organic growth that would be harder to achieve in a broader market.

Lastly, working within a niche allows you to become a recognized expert in your field. When you focus on serving a specific audience, you build authority and credibility within that space. Over time, this expertise can lead to additional opportunities, such as speaking engagements, collaborations, or partnerships. Being known as the go-to person for a particular niche not only helps you attract customers but also opens doors for growth and expansion as your reputation grows.

In conclusion, the power of niche markets for solopreneurs lies in their ability to focus on a specific audience, offer specialized expertise, and build deep customer loyalty. By identifying a niche that aligns with your strengths and has demand in the marketplace, you can position yourself as an expert and create a profitable business that stands out in a crowded landscape. Niche markets allow solopreneurs to compete effectively with larger businesses, charge premium prices, and create meaningful connections with customers who appreciate the value of personalized products and services. Embracing the potential of a niche market can be the key to long-term success as a solopreneur.

Inspiring Examples of Successful Solopreneurs

Solopreneurship has gained tremendous traction in recent years, with countless individuals finding success by building businesses on their own terms. The rise of technology, social media, and online platforms has allowed solopreneurs to break traditional business molds, creating thriving ventures with little more than a laptop, creativity, and hard work. Looking at inspiring examples of successful solopreneurs can offer valuable insights into what's possible and how others have navigated the path to success. These stories reflect the diversity of solopreneurship, from digital content creators to craftsmen to service providers, each building businesses that align with their passions and expertise.

One of the most well-known examples of a successful solopreneur is **Marie Forleo**, a life coach, entrepreneur, and bestselling author who has built an empire around empowering others to create lives and businesses they love. Marie's success story began with her creating content online and coaching clients one-on-one. Through her blog, online videos, and eventually her course "B-School," she has helped thousands of aspiring entrepreneurs launch and grow their businesses. What sets Marie apart is her authentic and relatable approach. She shares her own struggles and successes openly, connecting with her audience on a personal level. Marie's journey shows how a solopreneur can use digital platforms to build a highly successful, scalable business by offering value and forming a loyal community around their brand.

Another example is **Pat Flynn**, who is known for his blog, podcast, and online courses focused on passive income and online business strategies. Pat's solopreneurship journey began after he lost his job during the 2008 economic downturn. Instead of returning to a traditional career, he turned to the internet to find a way to support himself. He started a blog called Smart Passive Income, where he documented his efforts to build an online business. Over time, his transparent approach and willingness to share both his successes and failures attracted a large audience. Through his website, podcasts, and online products, Pat has generated multiple streams of income, proving that it's possible to create a sustainable business as a solopreneur by sharing knowledge and helping others achieve their goals.

Seth Godin is another inspiring example, particularly for those interested in content creation and thought leadership. Seth is an author, marketer, and public speaker who has written over 20 bestselling books, including "Purple Cow" and "The Dip." His blog, which has been running for over two decades, is one of the most popular marketing blogs in the world. Seth's ability to distill complex marketing and leadership concepts into simple, actionable advice has set him apart in the crowded online space. What makes Seth's journey as a solopreneur remarkable is his focus on building a personal brand around his unique voice and insights. He has shown that by consistently creating valuable content, you can build a loyal following and position yourself as a thought leader in your industry.

For those interested in physical products, **Sarah Kauss**, the founder of S'well, is a powerful example of how one person's vision can revolutionize a market. Sarah launched S'well in 2010 with the mission of reducing plastic waste by creating stylish, insulated water bottles. What began as a solo venture has grown into a globally recognized brand.

Sarah's success lies in her ability to combine her passion for environmental sustainability with a keen eye for design, creating a product that not only solves a practical problem but also resonates with a fashion-conscious audience. While S'well eventually grew beyond solopreneurship as the company expanded, Sarah's early journey exemplifies the power of a single person with a clear vision and dedication to creating a product that stands out.

For solopreneurs in the creative space, **Lisa Congdon**, an artist, illustrator, and author, offers an inspiring story of turning passion into a full-time career. Lisa started her art career later in life, pursuing illustration in her 30s with no formal training. Through her unique style, she gained attention and built a successful business selling her art, collaborating with brands, and publishing books. What makes Lisa's journey remarkable is her openness about the realities of being a creative entrepreneur, including the challenges and the importance of staying true to one's artistic vision. She built her business from the ground up, showing how solopreneurs in the arts can thrive by carving out their own space in the industry and building an authentic personal brand.

Gina Horkey, a freelance writer turned online educator, is another excellent example of a solopreneur who turned her skills into a profitable online business. Gina started as a freelance writer but quickly expanded her offerings to include virtual assistant services. As her business grew, she launched Horkey HandBook, an online resource for freelancers and virtual assistants looking to start and grow their businesses.

Gina's story is a testament to how solopreneurs can leverage their skills to not only provide services but also teach others how to succeed in similar fields. By identifying a gap in the market and providing the tools and education others need, she built a business that has helped countless solopreneurs find their own success.

Paul Jarvis is another solopreneur who has built a successful career around creating value for others. Paul is a web designer, writer, and creator of Fathom Analytics, a privacy-focused web analytics tool. He's also the author of the book "Company of One," which promotes the idea that bigger isn't always better when it comes to business. Paul's philosophy revolves around maintaining a small, sustainable business that aligns with his values and lifestyle. His work shows that solopreneurs don't need to scale into massive enterprises to find success. Instead, Paul focuses on providing high-quality products and content while maintaining control over his time and work. His journey is particularly inspiring for solopreneurs who value minimalism and sustainability in business.

In the fitness and wellness space, **Kayla Itsines** is a prime example of how a solopreneur can build a global brand by leveraging social media. Kayla, a personal trainer from Australia, gained a massive following on Instagram by sharing workout tips and transformations from her clients. She then launched the "Bikini Body Guide" (BBG) and an accompanying fitness app, which quickly became popular worldwide. Kayla's success lies in her ability to connect with her audience, provide valuable content consistently, and use social proof to showcase the results of her programs.

What started as a solo venture quickly expanded, but Kayla remains the face and driving force behind her brand, showing how solopreneurs can scale their business by building a strong personal brand and leveraging online platforms.

Finally, **Tim Ferriss** is one of the most well-known solopreneurs who has built a personal empire around lifestyle design and productivity. With the release of his bestselling book "The 4-Hour Workweek," Tim introduced millions to the idea of optimizing work and life to achieve more with less effort. He has since expanded his brand into podcasting, angel investing, and more, all while maintaining his core philosophy of working smarter, not harder. Tim's solopreneur success is rooted in his ability to experiment, iterate, and share his findings with his audience. His transparency and willingness to test unconventional ideas have made him a trusted source of inspiration for aspiring solopreneurs worldwide.

These examples of successful solopreneurs demonstrate the diversity of paths that can lead to success. From creating digital products to building personal brands, crafting physical goods, or offering specialized services, the opportunities are endless for solopreneurs who are willing to put in the work and stay true to their vision. What unites these stories is a common thread of passion, perseverance, and a deep understanding of their audience's needs. Solopreneurs have the advantage of agility and personal connection, which can be incredibly powerful in today's ever-evolving market. By learning from the successes of others, aspiring solopreneurs can find inspiration, guidance, and practical strategies to forge their own paths to success.

Real-Life Success Stories: Products That Changed the Game

Throughout history, innovative products created by solopreneurs and small businesses have changed industries and shaped consumer behavior. These success stories demonstrate how a single person with a vision, a deep understanding of their market, and the determination to bring a new idea to life can make an enormous impact. The following real-life success stories showcase products that not only achieved commercial success but also transformed the way people think about and use products.

One of the most iconic solopreneur success stories is that of **Sara Blakely**, the founder of **Spanx**. Sara Blakely's journey began with a simple idea: she wanted to create a more comfortable, flattering undergarment. Armed with a pair of scissors and a vision, she cut the feet off of a pair of pantyhose and quickly realized she was onto something that could revolutionize women's fashion. Without any formal design or business training, Sara invested her life savings into developing her product. After countless rejections from manufacturers, she eventually found a hosiery mill willing to take a chance on her idea. Spanx became an instant hit after Oprah Winfrey named it one of her "Favorite Things," and the rest is history. Sara's product not only reshaped the undergarment industry but also paved the way for other solopreneurs, proving that a great product idea can thrive even without the backing of a large corporation.

Another product that changed the game is the **GoPro** camera, invented by **Nick Woodman**. GoPro was born out of Nick's desire to capture high-quality action shots while surfing, something that traditional cameras couldn't do. After tinkering with prototypes and raising funds by selling belts out of his van, Nick launched the first GoPro camera, designed specifically for outdoor and action sports enthusiasts. What set GoPro apart was its ability to withstand extreme conditions while capturing stunning footage, something that quickly resonated with adrenaline junkies and adventure lovers around the world. GoPro didn't just create a product; it created a culture. The brand's cameras became synonymous with adventure, and user-generated content exploded on platforms like YouTube. Nick Woodman's journey from solopreneur to CEO of a publicly traded company demonstrates how a product that fills a gap in the market can become a global sensation.

In the world of health and wellness, **Melissa and Doug Bernstein** created a brand that has transformed how children play and learn. The duo started **Melissa & Doug**, a company that produces wooden toys and educational products, from their basement. They saw an opportunity to offer high-quality, educational toys that encouraged open-ended, imaginative play—something they felt was missing in the plastic, battery-operated toys that dominated the market. Their products, which include puzzles, pretend playsets, and art supplies, are designed to foster creativity, critical thinking, and motor skills in children. What started as a small, family-run business has grown into a globally recognized brand that is beloved by parents and educators alike. Melissa & Doug's success story highlights how solopreneurs can create products that align with their values and vision, filling a niche market with a meaningful, lasting impact.

Dollar Shave Club, founded by **Michael Dubin**, is another ground-breaking product that disrupted an entire industry. Michael's idea was simple yet revolutionary: offer men an affordable, subscription-based service for razors and grooming products. At the time, the razor market was dominated by a few large companies that sold expensive products, and consumers had little choice but to buy them. Dollar Shave Club offered an alternative, allowing customers to receive high-quality razors delivered to their doorsteps for a fraction of the price. The business took off after Michael's humorous and viral launch video captured the attention of millions of people online. Within a few years, Dollar Shave

Club had amassed millions of subscribers and was eventually acquired by Unilever for $1 billion. Michael's product not only solved a problem for consumers but also created an entirely new business model that other companies have since emulated.

In the beauty industry, **Emily Weiss**, the founder of **Glossier**, created a product line that has revolutionized how beauty brands interact with consumers. Emily started her career in the beauty industry as a blogger, running a popular site called Into The Gloss. Through her blog, she developed a deep understanding of what consumers wanted in their beauty products—simplicity, effectiveness, and transparency. Armed with this knowledge, she launched Glossier, a direct-to-consumer beauty brand focused on skincare and makeup essentials. What made Glossier stand out was its strong connection with its community. Emily prioritized listening to her audience, incorporating their feedback into product development, and fostering a sense of belonging among her customers. Glossier's minimalist packaging, "skin-first" approach, and direct engagement with consumers resonated deeply in the beauty industry, and the company grew into a billion-dollar business. Emily's story demonstrates the power of building a brand that centers around understanding and involving your audience in every step of the process.

Another innovative product that changed the game is the **Ring** doorbell, invented by **Jamie Siminoff**. Jamie, a serial inventor, was working on various projects in his garage when he came up with the idea for a video doorbell that allowed homeowners to see who was at their door via their smartphones. At the time, there wasn't much technology in the market focused on home security that was affordable and easy to use. After creating the prototype and naming it DoorBot, Jamie appeared on the television show "Shark Tank" to pitch his product. Although he didn't receive an investment, the exposure helped him get his product off the ground. He rebranded the company as Ring and continued to improve the technology. Ring became a household name, transforming home security by making it more accessible and affordable for everyday consumers. In 2018, Amazon acquired Ring for over $1 billion, and it continues to be a leader in the smart home security space.

One of the most impactful product success stories in the tech world is **Slack**, the communication platform created by **Stewart Butterfield**. Slack started as a side project during the development of a gaming company, but it quickly became clear that the internal communication tool they had created had far greater potential than the game itself. Slack transformed how teams and companies communicate by offering an intuitive, flexible platform that integrated with other essential business tools.

WHAT MADE SLACK STAND out was its focus on improving the efficiency of communication, reducing the need for endless email threads, and promoting real-time collaboration. As a result, Slack became an indispensable tool for businesses of all sizes, growing from a small internal project to a multi-billion-dollar company. Stewart's story shows how solopreneurs and small teams can pivot from their original ideas to discover new opportunities with game-changing potential.

Finally, **Jeni Britton Bauer**, the founder of **Jeni's Splendid Ice Creams**, is an inspiring example from the world of food and artisanal products. Jeni's story began with her love for making ice cream and a desire to create flavors that were unique, high-quality, and made from the best ingredients. She started by experimenting with flavor combinations and textures in her home kitchen, using whole ingredients and traditional methods that set her ice creams apart from the mass-produced options available in grocery stores. Her focus on quality and creativity—featuring flavors like Salty Caramel and Brambleberry Crisp—quickly gained her a loyal following. What started as a small ice cream shop in Ohio has grown into a nationwide brand with products sold in hundreds of stores across the U.S. Jeni's success shows that by offering something special and staying true to your craft, you can create a product that stands out even in a crowded market.

These real-life success stories demonstrate the incredible potential of solopreneurship and product innovation. Whether creating an entirely new category, disrupting an existing market, or simply improving upon a traditional concept, these products didn't just achieve commercial success—they changed the game. Each of these entrepreneurs identified a gap in the market, developed a product that offered a unique solution, and built a brand that resonated with their audience. By focusing on quality, creativity, and understanding their customers, these solopreneurs turned their ideas into iconic products that continue to make an impact today.

How to Start and Run a Business from Your Laptop

Starting and running a business from your laptop is not only possible but has become increasingly accessible thanks to advancements in technology, digital tools, and online platforms. Solopreneurs from all over the world are launching successful ventures with just a computer and an internet connection, creating businesses that offer them flexibility, independence, and the potential for global reach. Whether you want to start an online store, offer services, or create digital products, the key to success lies in your ability to harness the power of digital tools, stay organized, and stay connected to your audience. Here's how you can start and run a business from your laptop.

Define Your Business Idea and Niche

Before diving into the logistics of setting up your business, the first step is to clearly define your business idea. What kind of product or service will you offer? This might involve identifying a personal skill, passion, or area of expertise that you can monetize. For example, you could offer freelance writing or graphic design services, sell handmade crafts through an online marketplace, or create an online course that teaches others a valuable skill.

Once you have your idea, narrow it down to a specific niche. Trying to appeal to everyone is difficult and can dilute your efforts. Instead, think about the exact audience you want to serve and how your product or service will meet their needs. Defining your niche will make it easier to target your marketing, create focused content, and connect with your ideal customers.

Choose the Right Business Model

The beauty of running a business from your laptop is that there are several different business models to choose from, depending on your skills and goals. Some popular options include:

Freelance services: Offering services such as writing, design, marketing, or consulting is one of the simplest ways to start a business online. Freelancing requires minimal upfront investment and can be done entirely through digital platforms.

E-commerce: You can start an online store selling physical or digital products. Platforms like Shopify, Etsy, and Amazon make it easy to set up an e-commerce site without needing technical expertise.

Online courses: If you have expertise in a specific subject, you can create and sell online courses. Platforms like Teachable, Udemy, and Skillshare offer tools for creating, hosting, and selling courses to a global audience.

Digital products: Consider selling digital goods such as e-books, design templates, photography, or software. These products are easily scalable and can be sold repeatedly with no additional production costs.

Affiliate marketing: If you have a blog, YouTube channel, or large social media following, you can earn commissions by promoting products or services from other companies through affiliate marketing.

Set up Your Online Presence

Your online presence is the foundation of your business, and it all starts with a website. Having a professional website not only makes your business appear credible but also serves as the central hub where customers can learn about your offerings and interact with your brand.

There are several tools and platforms that make it easy to set up a website without needing advanced coding skills. Platforms like WordPress, Squarespace, and Wix offer drag-and-drop builders and templates that allow you to create a professional-looking website in just a few hours.

When building your website, be sure to include:

Clear branding: Use your website to communicate who you are, what you offer, and why customers should choose you. Your brand's voice, design, and messaging should reflect your business's unique personality and value proposition.

Portfolio or product pages: If you're offering services, include a portfolio or case studies that showcase your best work. For product-based businesses, make sure your product pages are easy to navigate and include high-quality images and descriptions.

Contact information: Make it easy for potential customers or clients to get in touch with you. This could include a contact form, email address, or links to your social media profiles.

If you're selling products, you'll also need an e-commerce platform to handle payments, inventory, and order fulfillment. Shopify, WooCommerce (for WordPress users), and BigCommerce are popular options that integrate seamlessly with your website.

Leverage Digital Tools for Business Operations

One of the main benefits of running a business from your laptop is the ability to automate and streamline operations with digital tools. Here are some essential tools that can help you manage your business efficiently:

Project management: Tools like Trello, Asana, or Monday.com allow you to organize your tasks, manage projects, and track deadlines. These platforms help keep you organized and on top of your workload, especially if you're managing multiple clients or projects.

Accounting and invoicing: For handling payments, expenses, and invoicing, tools like QuickBooks, FreshBooks, or Wave are great for small businesses. These tools simplify bookkeeping, help you keep track of finances, and ensure you get paid on time.

Email marketing: To communicate with your customers and build relationships, email marketing is essential. Tools like Mailchimp, ConvertKit, and ActiveCampaign allow you to create email campaigns, manage subscribers, and send automated messages.

Social media management: If you're promoting your business on social media, platforms like Hootsuite, Buffer, and Later allow you to schedule posts, track analytics, and manage multiple accounts in one place.

By using these digital tools, you can free up time and focus more on growing your business rather than getting bogged down in administrative tasks.

Market Your Business Online

Once your business is set up, it's time to focus on attracting customers. Since your business is entirely online, digital marketing will be your most powerful tool for generating traffic and sales. Here are a few strategies to consider:

Social media marketing: Platforms like Instagram, Facebook, LinkedIn, and Twitter are ideal for promoting your business, engaging with your audience, and building your brand. Choose the platform that best fits your target audience and regularly post content that's valuable, entertaining, or educational to your followers.

Content marketing: Creating blog posts, videos, podcasts, or other types of content that offer value to your audience is a great way to attract traffic to your website. Content marketing helps establish you as an authority in your niche and can drive organic traffic through search engine optimization (SEO).

Paid advertising: Consider using Google Ads or social media advertising to drive traffic to your website or landing pages. These platforms allow you to target specific demographics, interests, and behaviors, making it easier to reach your ideal customers.

Networking and outreach: Don't underestimate the power of networking, even in the digital space. Reach out to potential clients, collaborators, or influencers in your industry. Building relationships and word-of-mouth referrals can lead to new business opportunities.

Email marketing: Build an email list of subscribers and customers who are interested in your business. Sending regular updates, promotions, or valuable content via email is an effective way to nurture relationships and encourage repeat business.

Manage Your Time and Productivity

Running a business from your laptop offers immense flexibility, but it also requires discipline and effective time management. Since you don't have a traditional office environment to keep you on track, it's crucial to establish a routine that keeps you productive without feeling overwhelmed.

Set clear goals: Break your larger business objectives into smaller, actionable tasks. Create daily or weekly to-do lists to keep yourself focused and on track.

Create a schedule: Establish a work schedule that suits your lifestyle but ensures you're dedicating enough time to grow your business. Whether you work a traditional 9-to-5 schedule or prefer working in blocks of time throughout the day, consistency is key.

Avoid distractions: Working from a laptop means you're always one click away from distractions like social media, online shopping, or news. Use tools like StayFocusd or RescueTime to limit distractions and stay productive.

Take breaks: Burnout is a real risk when running a business solo. Schedule regular breaks throughout the day to recharge, exercise, or spend time away from your laptop.

Scale Your Business

As your laptop-based business grows, you may want to explore opportunities to scale. This could involve automating more tasks, hiring virtual assistants or freelancers, or expanding your offerings. The key to scaling successfully is to ensure that your business remains sustainable and that you maintain a healthy work-life balance.

By leveraging technology, digital marketing, and automation, you can expand your business without sacrificing quality or control. You can also explore new revenue streams, such as offering higher-tier services, launching new products, or developing strategic partnerships.

Conclusion

Starting and running a business from your laptop offers unparalleled freedom and flexibility, allowing you to pursue your passions, reach a global audience, and build a business on your own terms. By defining your business idea, setting up your online presence, utilizing digital tools, and implementing effective marketing strategies, you can create a successful venture that operates entirely from your laptop. The key to success is staying organized, disciplined, and connected to your audience while continuously adapting to new trends and opportunities. Whether you're just starting out or looking to scale, running a laptop-based business can offer endless possibilities for growth and fulfillment.

Creating a Productive Workspace for Your Solopreneur Venture

Creating a productive workspace is essential for any solopreneur, especially when you're running your business from home or any other flexible location. While working from a laptop offers the freedom to work from virtually anywhere, having a dedicated, well-organized workspace can greatly enhance your productivity, focus, and overall success. Whether you're working from a home office, a co-working space, or a corner of your living room, setting up a workspace that promotes efficiency and creativity is key to managing your tasks and growing your solopreneur venture.

Choose the Right Location

The first step to creating a productive workspace is choosing the right location. If you're working from home, designate a specific area where you can work consistently. Ideally, this should be a quiet, distraction-free zone where you can focus on your tasks. Avoid working from your bed or couch, as these areas are associated with relaxation and can make it harder to maintain a productive mindset.

If you don't have a separate room to dedicate as a home office, try to carve out a corner of a bedroom, living room, or dining area that can be used solely for work. Having a specific place where you work each day can help mentally signal that it's time to focus, which improves concentration and efficiency.

If you prefer working outside the home, consider finding a local co-working space or a café that provides a comfortable environment. Co-working spaces are particularly beneficial because they offer networking opportunities, high-speed internet, and other business-related amenities. Wherever you decide to set up, make sure it's a space that makes you feel motivated and focused.

Invest in Ergonomics

Ergonomics play a crucial role in your long-term productivity and comfort. Sitting in an uncomfortable position for long hours can lead to fatigue, back pain, and poor posture, all of which can negatively affect your focus and health. To avoid this, invest in a good-quality ergonomic chair and desk setup that promotes a healthy posture.

When setting up your workspace, ensure that your laptop or computer screen is at eye level so you're not straining your neck. If you're working from a laptop, consider using a laptop stand, external keyboard, and mouse to create a more ergonomic setup. Additionally, your feet should rest flat on the floor or on a footrest, and your arms should be positioned at a comfortable angle when typing.

Taking the time to invest in ergonomic furniture and equipment may require some upfront costs, but it will pay off in the long run by helping you avoid discomfort and potential health issues. A comfortable workspace also makes it easier to focus on your work without being distracted by physical discomfort.

ORGANIZE YOUR WORKSPACE

Clutter can quickly derail your productivity, so it's important to keep your workspace organized and free of distractions. Start by decluttering your desk and removing any unnecessary items. Only keep the essentials—such as your laptop, notebooks, pens, and any other tools you use regularly—on your desk. Use storage solutions like shelves, drawers, or desk organizers to keep things neat and easily accessible.

If you're someone who thrives in a minimalist environment, try to keep your workspace clean and simple. However, if you find that a few personal items like photos, plants, or motivational quotes help inspire you, don't hesitate to include them in your setup. The goal is to create a workspace that feels organized but also inviting and personalized to your taste.

To further streamline your workflow, consider using digital organization tools. For example, tools like Trello, Evernote, or Google Drive can help you organize files, notes, and projects, reducing the need for physical paper clutter. By keeping both your physical and digital workspace organized, you can reduce distractions and improve your overall focus.

Optimize Lighting

Lighting plays a significant role in your productivity. Poor lighting can strain your eyes, cause headaches, and make you feel tired or sluggish. On the other hand, proper lighting can improve your focus, reduce eye strain, and boost your mood.

If possible, set up your workspace near a source of natural light, such as a window. Natural light has been shown to improve concentration and overall well-being. However, if natural light isn't available, invest in good quality artificial lighting. Opt for soft, warm lighting that mimics natural light, and avoid harsh fluorescent lights that can cause discomfort over time.

Task lighting, such as a desk lamp, can also be helpful for illuminating specific areas where you need extra focus, like your keyboard or workspace. Make sure your lighting is bright enough to keep you alert but not so bright that it causes glare on your screen.

Minimize Distractions

Distractions can significantly impact your productivity, so it's important to create a workspace that minimizes potential interruptions. If you're working from home and have family members or roommates around, communicate your working hours to them and set boundaries to reduce disturbances.

To minimize digital distractions, use apps like Focus@Will, Freedom, or RescueTime to block distracting websites and social media during work hours. You can also set your phone to "Do Not Disturb" mode to avoid being interrupted by notifications or calls.

If noise is an issue in your environment, invest in noise-canceling headphones or use a white noise machine to create a quieter, more focused atmosphere. Alternatively, listen to calming music or instrumental playlists designed to boost concentration.

Incorporate Elements That Boost Motivation

Your workspace should not only be functional but also inspire you to stay motivated and creative. Surround yourself with elements that remind you of your goals and achievements. This could be a vision board, a framed quote, or even a list of short-term and long-term goals that you want to achieve in your solopreneur journey.

Consider adding plants to your workspace, as they can improve air quality and create a calming, positive environment. Studies have shown that having greenery in your workspace can reduce stress and increase productivity.

Additionally, personalize your space with items that reflect your personality and bring you joy. Whether it's artwork, photos of loved ones, or souvenirs from travels, creating a workspace that feels uniquely yours can make it a more enjoyable place to spend time in and help you stay motivated during long work hours.

Establish a Routine

Your workspace is most effective when paired with a solid routine. Set regular working hours that you can stick to each day. This helps create a sense of structure, even when working from home, and ensures that you dedicate enough time to your solopreneur tasks.

Start each day by organizing your tasks and setting clear priorities. Tools like Asana or Todoist can help you manage your to-do lists and track your progress on specific projects. Taking a few minutes at the beginning of each day to review your goals and outline your most important tasks can help you stay focused and productive throughout the day.

Make sure to schedule breaks as well. Working for extended periods without breaks can lead to burnout and reduced efficiency. Try using the Pomodoro Technique, which involves working for 25 minutes and then taking a 5-minute break, or find a rhythm that works best for your focus levels. Breaks give you a chance to recharge and return to your work with fresh energy.

Leverage Technology for Productivity

Leveraging technology is key to optimizing your workspace as a solopreneur. Beyond basic tools like project management apps and communication platforms, consider using software that automates repetitive tasks. For example, if you're running an e-commerce business, tools like Zapier can automate order confirmations, follow-up emails, and social media posts.

Productivity tools like Notion, Slack, and Google Workspace can streamline collaboration and organization, even if you're working alone. These tools help you keep track of important documents, projects, and communications in one place, reducing the clutter and confusion that can come with managing a solopreneur business.

Prioritize Health and Well-Being

Lastly, don't overlook the importance of maintaining your health and well-being while working from your laptop. Incorporate movement into your daily routine to avoid the negative effects of sitting for long periods. Consider using a standing desk or taking regular stretch breaks to keep your energy levels up. Simple stretches or short walks can improve circulation and prevent fatigue.

Make sure you're staying hydrated and eating healthy snacks to maintain your focus throughout the day. Keeping a water bottle at your desk is a simple way to remind yourself to stay hydrated.

Mental well-being is equally important, so make time for activities that reduce stress, such as meditation, deep breathing exercises, or journaling. A healthy, well-balanced routine will keep your mind sharp and help you maintain the energy you need to run your solopreneur venture successfully.

Creating a productive workspace for your solopreneur venture is essential to your success. By choosing the right location, investing in ergonomic furniture, staying organized, and minimizing distractions, you can optimize your environment for maximum efficiency and focus. Incorporating elements that inspire and motivate you will make your workspace a place where you enjoy spending time, helping you stay committed to your goals. When combined with the right technology, a structured routine, and a focus on your well-being, your workspace will become a powerful tool that supports your solopreneur journey.

Mastering Time Management as a Solopreneur

Mastering time management as a solopreneur is one of the most critical skills you can develop to ensure the success of your business. Without the structure of a traditional office or team, it's easy to get overwhelmed by the sheer volume of tasks that need to be done, from marketing and customer service to product development and bookkeeping. As a solopreneur, you wear many hats, and your ability to effectively manage your time will determine how efficiently you can run your business, meet your goals, and maintain a healthy work-life balance. Here are strategies for mastering time management as a solopreneur.

Set Clear Goals

The first step in effective time management is having a clear understanding of your short-term and long-term goals. Without clear goals, it's easy to spend your time on tasks that don't directly contribute to the growth of your business. Start by defining your larger business objectives—these could be revenue targets, product launches, or expanding your customer base. Once you have those in place, break them down into smaller, actionable tasks that you can work on day by day.

Setting clear goals not only gives you a sense of direction but also helps you prioritize tasks based on their importance and impact. When you know exactly what you're working toward, you can allocate your time more effectively and ensure that the majority of your efforts are focused on activities that move your business forward.

Prioritize Your Tasks

With multiple responsibilities on your plate, prioritizing your tasks is crucial. The key is to identify which tasks are the most important and will have the greatest impact on your business. One useful tool for prioritizing is the **Eisenhower Matrix**, which helps you categorize tasks based on urgency and importance:

Urgent and important: Tasks that need to be done immediately and are critical for your business, such as responding to client inquiries or completing a time-sensitive project.

Important but not urgent: Tasks that contribute to your long-term success, such as planning marketing strategies, working on product development, or improving your skills. These tasks should be scheduled, as they are essential for growth.

Urgent but not important: Tasks that may need attention but don't significantly impact your goals. These could be delegated or streamlined if possible.

Not urgent and not important: Tasks that are distractions or time-wasters. These should be minimized or eliminated altogether.

By prioritizing your tasks in this way, you'll be able to focus on what matters most and avoid getting caught up in busy work that doesn't push your business forward.

Create a Daily Schedule

A well-structured daily schedule can make a world of difference in how productive you are as a solopreneur. Start by creating a routine that you can follow each day. This routine should include dedicated time blocks for essential tasks like client work, marketing, administrative duties, and personal time. Structuring your day helps you maintain consistency and ensures that you're devoting the right amount of time to each aspect of your business.

To make your schedule more effective, use time-blocking techniques where you assign specific hours of your day to particular tasks or categories of work. For instance, you could block off 9:00 a.m. to 11:00 a.m. for deep work on a project, 11:00 a.m. to 12:00 p.m. for emails and client communication, and 1:00 p.m. to 3:00 p.m. for marketing activities. By breaking your day into focused time blocks, you can concentrate on one task at a time and avoid multitasking, which often leads to reduced productivity.

Use the Pomodoro Technique

The **Pomodoro Technique** is a time management method designed to increase focus and productivity by breaking your work into intervals, traditionally 25 minutes in length, followed by a 5-minute break. After completing four "Pomodoros," take a longer break of 15 to 30 minutes.

This technique is particularly useful for solopreneurs because it helps you maintain intense focus on a task for a set period without distractions. The frequent short breaks prevent burnout and help you stay energized throughout the day. It's especially helpful for tasks that require sustained concentration, such as writing, designing, or developing new products. Using a timer or a dedicated Pomodoro app can make it easier to implement this technique in your daily routine.

Eliminate Distractions

Distractions are one of the biggest challenges when running a business from your laptop, especially if you're working from home. To manage your time effectively, it's crucial to minimize distractions that can pull you away from your work. Common distractions include social media, phone notifications, and non-work-related tasks.

To eliminate distractions, start by turning off non-essential notifications on your phone and computer during work hours. You can use apps like **Focus@Will**, **RescueTime**, or **Freedom** to block distracting websites and apps while you're working. Additionally, if you live with family members or roommates, communicate your work schedule to them so they know when you're unavailable.

Creating a dedicated workspace where you can focus is also important. Even if you don't have a separate room for an office, setting up a consistent work area helps mentally separate work from personal life, reducing the temptation to be distracted.

AUTOMATE REPETITIVE Tasks

One of the best ways to save time as a solopreneur is to automate repetitive or time-consuming tasks. There are numerous tools and apps available that can automate various aspects of your business, from social media scheduling to email marketing.

For example:

Hootsuite or **Buffer** can help automate your social media posts, allowing you to schedule content in advance.

Zapier can automate workflows between apps, such as automatically sending follow-up emails when a customer purchases a product.

Mailchimp or **ConvertKit** can automate email sequences, such as welcome emails for new subscribers or abandoned cart reminders for e-commerce businesses.

By automating tasks that don't require manual intervention, you can free up time for more strategic and creative aspects of your business.

Learn to Delegate

As a solopreneur, you may feel like you need to handle everything yourself, but trying to do it all can lead to burnout and inefficiency. Delegating tasks that don't require your direct involvement can be a game-changer for your time management.

If you're in a position to outsource work, consider hiring freelancers or virtual assistants to take over tasks like customer service, bookkeeping, graphic design, or social media management. Platforms like **Upwork**, **Fiverr**, and

Freelancer make it easy to find skilled professionals for specific tasks, allowing you to focus on the areas where you can add the most value.

Even if you're not ready to hire help, you can delegate some tasks to software tools, such as automating your invoicing or using customer relationship management (CRM) systems to handle client communications.

Set Boundaries between Work and Personal Life

One of the challenges solopreneurs face is the blurring of lines between work and personal life, especially if you're working from home. Without clear boundaries, it's easy to overwork or find yourself doing personal errands during work hours. Setting boundaries ensures that you remain productive during work hours while also protecting your time for rest and relaxation.

To create these boundaries, establish set working hours that you stick to each day. When your workday ends, make a conscious effort to disconnect from work—turn off your computer, stop checking emails, and shift your focus to personal time. This separation helps prevent burnout and ensures you're recharged for the next day's tasks.

Review and Reflect on Your Productivity

A key component of mastering time management is regularly reviewing your productivity. At the end of each week, take time to reflect on what you accomplished, what challenges you faced, and how effectively you managed your time. Did you meet your goals? Were there any tasks that took longer than expected or areas where you got side-tracked?

This reflection allows you to make adjustments to your workflow, optimize your daily schedule, and identify habits that need improvement. Over time, this practice will help you become more efficient and aware of how you're using your time.

Take Breaks and Maintain Balance

Effective time management isn't just about squeezing the most work into each day—it's also about maintaining a healthy balance between productivity and rest. Taking regular breaks throughout your workday, as well as scheduling time for self-care, exercise, and hobbies, is essential for long-term success. Overworking can lead to burnout, which will ultimately slow down your productivity.

Consider implementing the **Pomodoro Technique** or taking scheduled breaks during the day. Additionally, make sure you're getting enough sleep, eating well, and finding time for activities outside of work that bring you joy. A balanced approach to work and life will keep you energized, creative, and focused in the long run.

Mastering time management as a solopreneur is crucial for ensuring that you stay productive, meet your business goals, and maintain a healthy work-life balance. By setting clear goals, prioritizing tasks, creating a daily schedule, and minimizing distractions, you can optimize your time and make the most of each workday. Leveraging technology, automating repetitive tasks, and outsourcing when possible will help you free up time for the strategic aspects of your business. Remember to review your productivity regularly, take breaks, and maintain balance to ensure long-term success as a solopreneur. By developing strong time management habits, you can work more efficiently and create a thriving business that supports your vision and goals.

Marketing Your Solopreneur Business in the Digital World

Marketing your solopreneur business in the digital world is a powerful way to reach a broad audience, build brand awareness, and grow your customer base. As a solopreneur, you likely have limited resources and time, making it essential to adopt marketing strategies that are both effective and efficient. Fortunately, the digital landscape offers a variety of tools and platforms that can help you market your business without needing a huge budget or team. From social media marketing to content creation, email campaigns, and SEO, digital marketing enables solopreneurs to compete with larger businesses on a level playing field.

Build a Strong Online Presence

Your online presence is the foundation of your digital marketing strategy, and it starts with your website. Your website is often the first point of contact for potential customers, so it needs to clearly convey who you are, what you offer, and why they should choose you. Make sure your site is easy to navigate, visually appealing, and optimized for mobile users since many people access websites on their smartphones.

Key elements to include on your website:

Clear branding: Your website should reflect your business's personality and values, with a consistent tone, style, and message that resonates with your target audience.

About page: This is where visitors can learn more about you, your background, and your mission. Since you're a solopreneur, this page helps build a personal connection with potential customers by telling your story.

Services or product pages: Clearly describe what you offer, highlighting the benefits and value your customers will receive. If you offer multiple services or products, create dedicated pages for each.

Call-to-action (CTA): Every page of your website should include a CTA that encourages visitors to take the next step, whether it's signing up for your newsletter, booking a consultation, or making a purchase.

Contact information: Make it easy for potential customers to reach you. Include your email, phone number, or a contact form on your website so visitors can get in touch with you directly.

Leverage Social Media for Marketing

Social media is one of the most powerful tools for marketing your solopreneur business in the digital world. Platforms like Instagram, Facebook, LinkedIn, and Twitter allow you to engage directly with your target audience, build relationships, and showcase your products or services.

TO EFFECTIVELY USE social media for marketing:

Choose the right platform: Focus on the platforms where your target audience is most active. For example, if you're a visual brand or sell physical products, Instagram might be ideal. If you offer professional services, LinkedIn might be more effective.

Create consistent content: Post regularly to keep your audience engaged. Share behind-the-scenes content, tips, tutorials, testimonials, or product updates. Consistency helps build trust and keeps you top of mind for your audience.

Engage with your audience: Social media is about building relationships. Respond to comments, answer questions, and engage with your followers' posts. The more you interact, the more likely your audience is to feel connected to your brand.

Use hashtags: Hashtags help increase your visibility by making your content discoverable to people searching for related topics. Research popular hashtags in your niche and use them strategically in your posts.

Run paid ads: While organic social media marketing is important, running paid ads can help you reach a larger, more targeted audience. Social media platforms like Facebook and Instagram allow you to target ads based on demographics, interests, and behaviors, making it easier to connect with potential customers who are likely to be interested in your offerings.

Invest in Content Marketing

Content marketing involves creating valuable, relevant, and consistent content that attracts and engages your target audience. As a solopreneur, content marketing is a great way to showcase your expertise, build trust with potential customers, and drive traffic to your website.

Content marketing can take many forms, including:

Blog posts: Writing blog articles on topics related to your industry or business can help establish you as an authority in your niche. Blog posts can also improve your website's SEO, making it easier for potential customers to find you through search engines.

Videos: Video content is highly engaging and can be used to explain your product, demonstrate your services, or share customer testimonials. Platforms like YouTube and Instagram make it easy to create and share video content.

Podcasts: If you enjoy speaking and sharing insights, consider starting a podcast. Podcasting allows you to build an audience and share your expertise in a format that's convenient for your listeners.

Infographics: Infographics are visually engaging and help simplify complex information. They're perfect for sharing statistics, processes, or step-by-step guides and can be distributed on social media or your blog.

E-books and guides: Creating in-depth content like e-books or guides allows you to provide more detailed information to your audience. You can use this content to capture leads by offering it in exchange for email signups.

The key to content marketing is consistency. Create a content calendar and stick to a schedule, whether it's posting weekly blog articles, monthly videos, or daily social media updates. Over time, your content will help build a loyal audience and position you as a trusted expert in your field.

Utilize Email Marketing

Email marketing is a powerful tool for nurturing relationships with your audience and converting leads into customers. It allows you to communicate directly with people who are already interested in your business and provide them with personalized offers, updates, and valuable content.

To get started with email marketing:

Build an email list: Offer something valuable in exchange for email addresses, such as a free guide, discount code, or exclusive content. Make it easy for visitors to sign up by placing opt-in forms on your website and social media channels.

Segment your audience: As your email list grows, segment it based on customer preferences, behaviors, or demographics. This allows you to send more targeted emails that are relevant to each group, increasing the likelihood of engagement.

Create engaging campaigns: Your email content should be valuable and engaging. Send newsletters with updates, blog highlights, product promotions, or exclusive offers. Make sure your emails are visually appealing, mobile-friendly, and have a clear call to action.

Automate your emails: Use tools like Mailchimp, ConvertKit, or ActiveCampaign to automate your email marketing. You can set up sequences for new subscribers, send follow-up emails, and schedule campaigns in advance.

Optimize for Search Engines (SEO)

Search engine optimization (SEO) is the process of improving your website's visibility in search engine results. The higher your website ranks on Google and other search engines, the more likely potential customers are to find you when they search for relevant keywords.

To optimize your website for SEO:

Use relevant keywords: Conduct keyword research to find out what terms your target audience is searching for. Incorporate these keywords into your website's content, including page titles, headings, meta descriptions, and blog posts.

Create high-quality content: Search engines prioritize websites that provide valuable, well-written, and relevant content. Regularly publishing blog posts, articles, or videos that answer your audience's questions or solve their problems can improve your search rankings.

Optimize your website's performance: Ensure that your website loads quickly, is mobile-friendly, and provides a good user experience. Slow websites or sites that aren't optimized for mobile devices can negatively impact your rankings.

Build backlinks: Backlinks are links from other websites that point to your site. They signal to search engines that your content is valuable and trustworthy. You can build backlinks by guest blogging, collaborating with influencers, or getting your content featured on relevant websites.

SEO is a long-term strategy, but when done correctly, it can drive a steady stream of organic traffic to your website without requiring ongoing ad spend.

Collaborate with Influencers and Partners

Collaborating with influencers, bloggers, or other solopreneurs in your niche can help you expand your reach and attract new customers. Influencer marketing doesn't have to be limited to large corporations—many solopreneurs find success working with micro-influencers who have smaller but highly engaged audiences.

When collaborating with influencers or partners:

Find the right fit: Look for influencers or businesses that share your target audience and values. Collaborating with someone who resonates with your audience increases the chances of successful promotion.

Offer value: Make sure the collaboration offers value to both parties. This could be in the form of cross-promotion, product giveaways, or guest blog posts.

Be transparent: Ensure that both parties are clear about the terms of the collaboration, including expectations, deliverables, and compensation (if applicable).

Track and Analyze Your Results

Digital marketing is data-driven, so it's important to regularly track your results and analyze what's working and what's not. Use tools like **Google Analytics**, **Facebook Insights**, and your email marketing platform's analytics to measure key metrics such as website traffic, engagement, conversions, and ROI.

By monitoring these metrics, you can identify which strategies are driving the most traffic and sales, allowing you to focus on the tactics that deliver the best results. Regularly review your performance, adjust your marketing efforts as needed, and continue optimizing your strategy for maximum impact.

Marketing your solopreneur business in the digital world offers endless possibilities to grow your brand, attract new customers, and build a loyal following. By establishing a strong online presence, leveraging social media, creating valuable content, and using SEO and email marketing, you can effectively promote your business even with limited resources. Digital marketing is a dynamic and ever-evolving field, so be prepared to experiment with different strategies, track your progress, and adjust as needed. With dedication and the right approach, your solopreneur business can thrive in the competitive digital landscape.

Crafting a Brand That Resonates with Your Audience

Crafting a brand that resonates with your audience is one of the most important aspects of building a successful solopreneur business. Your brand is more than just a logo or a catchy tagline—it's the perception people have of your business and the emotional connection they feel with it. A well-crafted brand not only conveys your values, personality, and mission, but it also creates a meaningful relationship with your audience, making them more likely to choose your products or services over competitors. To build a brand that truly resonates, you must be authentic, understand your audience deeply, and consistently communicate your message through every touchpoint.

Define Your Brand's Purpose and Values

Before you can craft a brand that resonates, you need to clearly define your brand's purpose and values. Your brand's purpose is the "why" behind your business—what drives you to do what you do. It's more than just making a profit; it's about the impact you want to make and the value you offer to your customers. Think about what inspires you to run your business and how you want to make a difference in your customers' lives.

Your values, on the other hand, represent the principles that guide your business. These are the core beliefs that shape how you operate, how you interact with customers, and the type of experience you provide. For example, if you value sustainability, your brand may emphasize eco-friendly products or business practices. If you value creativity, your brand may focus on offering innovative solutions or unique designs.

When your audience shares your values, they are more likely to feel connected to your brand on a personal level. To define your brand's purpose and values, ask yourself the following questions:

Why did I start this business?

What do I hope to achieve beyond financial success?

What are the values that guide how I run my business and interact with my audience?

What do I want my brand to stand for in the minds of my customers?

Once you've defined your purpose and values, make sure they're communicated clearly across all aspects of your branding, from your website and social media to your product offerings and customer service.

Understand Your Audience

To craft a brand that resonates with your audience, you need to know exactly who they are and what matters most to them. This means going beyond basic demographics like age, gender, and location and delving into their preferences, needs, desires, and pain points.

The more you understand your audience, the better you can tailor your brand's message, products, and services to meet their specific needs. Here's how you can gain a deeper understanding of your audience:

Create buyer personas: A buyer persona is a semi-fictional representation of your ideal customer. Think about their goals, challenges, motivations, and what drives their purchasing decisions. Are they looking for convenience, quality, affordability, or innovation? Crafting detailed personas helps you keep your target audience in mind when making branding and marketing decisions.

Engage with your audience: One of the best ways to learn more about your audience is to engage with them directly. Use social media, surveys, or email newsletters to ask questions, gather feedback, and learn more about their needs. The insights you gain will help you shape a brand that aligns with their expectations.

Observe competitors: Look at how your competitors engage with their audiences and what resonates with them. Analyze their branding, messaging, and customer interactions to identify gaps or opportunities where your brand can stand out.

Understanding your audience enables you to create a brand that speaks directly to their needs and desires, making them feel like your business was made just for them.

Create a Unique Brand Identity

Your brand identity is the visual and verbal representation of your brand, and it includes everything from your logo and color scheme to your tone of voice and messaging. A strong brand identity helps differentiate you from competitors and creates a cohesive experience across all touchpoints, making it easier for your audience to recognize and remember your business.

Here's how to create a unique and memorable brand identity:

Logo: Your logo is often the first thing people associate with your brand. It should be simple, memorable, and reflective of your business's personality and values. If you're not a designer, consider working with a professional to create a logo that's timeless and versatile across different platforms.

Color scheme: Colors evoke emotions and play a significant role in how your brand is perceived. Choose a color palette that aligns with the feelings you want to evoke in your audience. For example, blue is often associated with trust and professionalism, while yellow conveys warmth and optimism. Use your brand colors consistently across your website, social media, packaging, and other materials.

Typography: Your choice of fonts should complement your brand's personality. Serif fonts often convey tradition and reliability, while sans-serif fonts are modern and clean. Choose fonts that are easy to read and align with the tone of your brand.

Voice and tone: Your brand's voice is how you communicate with your audience, while tone refers to how you adapt that voice depending on the context. Are you conversational and friendly, or professional and authoritative? Your tone should reflect your audience's preferences and how they like to be spoken to. For example, if you're a health coach catering to millennials, a conversational, upbeat tone might resonate more than a formal one.

Tagline or slogan: If you can summarize your brand's value proposition in a few words, a tagline can be a great addition to your brand identity. It should be clear, concise, and aligned with your brand's mission. For example, Nike's famous tagline "Just Do It" embodies their brand's focus on motivation and athleticism.

Be Authentic and Consistent

Authenticity is crucial for building a brand that resonates. In the digital age, consumers are savvy and can quickly detect inauthenticity. Trying to be something you're not or mimicking another brand's style can backfire, as it often comes across as disingenuous.

Instead, focus on being true to your brand's values, mission, and personality. Share your story, your challenges, and your successes. Being open and honest about your journey helps humanize your brand and makes it easier for your audience to connect with you on a deeper level. Authentic brands tend to foster loyalty because customers feel like they're supporting a business that aligns with their own values.

Consistency is equally important when it comes to building a strong brand. Every interaction a customer has with your business—from your website and social media to your emails and customer service—should reflect the same brand personality and message. Inconsistent branding can confuse your audience and weaken your brand's impact. Make sure your visuals, tone, and messaging are aligned across all platforms and channels to create a seamless brand experience.

Connect Emotionally with Your Audience

A brand that resonates with its audience goes beyond offering great products or services—it creates an emotional connection. People don't just buy products; they buy into the stories, values, and emotions associated with those products.

To create this emotional connection, focus on storytelling. Share your brand's journey, the challenges you've overcome, and the values that drive your business. Tell the story of why you started your business and how your products or services make a difference in the lives of your customers. Personal stories, customer testimonials, and case studies are all great ways to connect emotionally with your audience.

You can also create an emotional connection by focusing on the benefits and outcomes your audience will experience from your product or service. Instead of just highlighting features, explain how your offerings solve problems, improve lives, or bring joy. For example, a skincare brand might focus on how their products help customers feel more confident and comfortable in their skin, rather than just listing ingredients.

Foster Community and Engagement

Brands that resonate with their audience often go beyond transactions and build communities. By creating a sense of belonging, you can turn your customers into loyal advocates who are emotionally invested in your brand's success.

To foster community and engagement:

Engage on social media: Use social media platforms to interact with your audience, respond to their comments, and ask for their feedback. Social media is a powerful tool for building relationships and making your audience feel heard and valued.

Create user-generated content: Encourage your customers to share their experiences with your products or services through photos, reviews, or testimonials. Feature user-generated content on your website and social media channels to build social proof and strengthen your brand's community.

Offer exclusive content or perks: Reward your loyal customers with exclusive content, discounts, or early access to new products. By making your audience feel special and valued, you deepen their connection to your brand.

Host events or online challenges: Whether it's a live Q&A, a workshop, or an online challenge, hosting events can bring your audience together and provide them with value. These experiences create positive associations with your brand and encourage continued engagement.

Evolve with Your Audience

Your audience's needs and preferences will change over time, and your brand must evolve to stay relevant. Pay attention to trends in your industry and shifts in your audience's behavior. Keep the lines of communication open by regularly seeking feedback from your customers and adjusting your offerings and messaging as needed.

While it's important to stay true to your brand's core values, remaining adaptable allows you to grow with your audience and maintain a brand that continues to resonate in an ever-changing market.

Crafting a brand that resonates with your audience involves more than creating a great logo or catchy tagline. It's about defining your purpose, values, and identity, and communicating those consistently across all touchpoints. A brand that resonates with its audience doesn't just attract customers—it turns them into passionate advocates who share your story and believe in your mission.

Social Media Marketing for the Modern Solopreneur

Social media marketing has become a powerful tool for solopreneurs to connect with their audience, build their brand, and grow their business. With billions of people using platforms like Instagram, Facebook, LinkedIn, TikTok, and Twitter, social media offers an accessible and cost-effective way to reach potential customers, showcase products or services, and create meaningful engagement. The challenge for modern solopreneurs is figuring out how to navigate these platforms effectively while managing all the other aspects of running a business. Here's how to leverage social media marketing as a solopreneur to build your brand and attract customers.

Choose the Right Platforms for Your Business

Not all social media platforms are created equal, and as a solopreneur, it's important to focus your time and energy on the platforms that are most likely to yield results for your business. Each platform has a unique audience and type of content that performs best, so consider where your target audience spends their time and what kind of content you enjoy creating.

Here's a brief overview of the most popular platforms and what they're best suited for:

Instagram: Ideal for businesses with a strong visual component, such as fashion, fitness, food, or art. Instagram is also great for personal branding and storytelling through photos, videos, and Instagram Stories.

Facebook: With its massive user base, Facebook works well for a wide range of businesses. It's particularly effective for businesses targeting older demographics. Facebook also has powerful advertising tools for reaching specific audiences and engaging through Facebook Groups.

LinkedIn: Best for B2B businesses and solopreneurs offering professional services like consulting, coaching, or freelancing. LinkedIn is a platform for networking, sharing expertise, and connecting with potential clients or collaborators.

TikTok: Perfect for businesses that appeal to a younger demographic and those with creative, video-driven content. TikTok's short-form video format allows you to engage your audience in fun, relatable ways, making it especially useful for personal brands.

Twitter: Great for solopreneurs who want to engage in real-time conversations, share news, and offer quick insights. It's especially useful for businesses in tech, marketing, and media industries.

Pinterest: Ideal for solopreneurs offering visually driven products or services, especially in industries like home decor, fashion, DIY, or food. Pinterest users are often looking for inspiration, making it a great platform for showcasing products and driving traffic to your website.

DEVELOP A SOCIAL MEDIA Strategy

Before diving into social media marketing, it's essential to develop a clear strategy that aligns with your business goals. A well-thought-out strategy ensures that your efforts are focused, purposeful, and likely to generate results. Here's how to build an effective social media strategy:

Set specific goals: What do you want to achieve with social media marketing? Your goals could include increasing brand awareness, driving website traffic, generating leads, or growing your email list. Setting clear, measurable goals helps you stay focused and track your progress.

Identify your target audience: Who are you trying to reach? Consider your ideal customer's demographics, interests, and pain points. Knowing your audience allows you to tailor your content to their preferences and needs.

Plan your content: Content is the foundation of your social media strategy. Plan the types of content you'll create, such as blog posts, videos, tutorials, infographics, or behind-the-scenes updates. Ensure your content aligns with your brand and adds value to your audience.

Create a content calendar: Consistency is key to social media success. A content calendar helps you stay organized and ensures that you're posting regularly. Plan out your posts for the week or month ahead, including what you'll post, when you'll post it, and which platforms you'll use.

Mix up your content: Keep your audience engaged by varying the type of content you share. Combine educational posts (like tips or tutorials) with entertaining content (like memes or fun facts) and promotional posts (like product launches or sales). This variety ensures your social media feed doesn't feel too sales-focused.

Use analytics: Most social media platforms provide analytics that give you insight into how your posts are performing. Pay attention to metrics like engagement, reach, and clicks to see what's working and what's not. Use this data to adjust your strategy as needed.

Focus on Engagement, Not Just Promotion

One of the biggest mistakes solopreneurs make with social media marketing is focusing solely on promoting their products or services. While it's important to showcase what you offer, social media is ultimately about building relationships and fostering community.

Here's how to boost engagement on social media:

Respond to comments and messages: Make it a habit to respond to your followers' comments, messages, and mentions. Engaging in conversations shows that you're approachable and value their feedback, which helps build trust and loyalty.

Ask questions: Encourage interaction by asking your followers questions about their preferences, challenges, or experiences. This not only boosts engagement but also provides you with valuable insights about your audience.

Use polls and surveys: Many social media platforms, like Instagram and Twitter, have built-in tools for creating polls or surveys. Use these features to get quick feedback from your audience, which can help you shape your offerings and content.

Host giveaways or contests: Running a giveaway or contest can help increase your visibility and grow your following. Encourage users to enter by liking your post, tagging friends, or sharing your content. Just be sure that the prize is relevant to your business and appeals to your target audience.

Show your personality: People connect with people, not just brands. Show your face, share your journey, and let your personality shine through your content. Whether it's sharing a personal story, a funny anecdote, or a behind-the-scenes glimpse into your workday, authenticity goes a long way in building relationships with your audience.

Use Hashtags Strategically

Hashtags are an effective way to increase your visibility on social media platforms like Instagram, Twitter, and TikTok. When used strategically, hashtags can help you reach a broader audience and make your content discoverable to people who aren't already following you.

To use hashtags effectively:

Research popular hashtags: Look at what hashtags are commonly used in your industry or niche. You can use tools like Hashtagify or All Hashtag to find relevant hashtags that are trending or widely used by your audience.

Mix popular and niche hashtags: Popular hashtags can help you reach a large audience, but they can also be highly competitive. Niche hashtags, while smaller, often attract a more engaged and relevant audience. Use a combination of both to increase your chances of being discovered.

Create a branded hashtag: A branded hashtag is unique to your business and helps build a community around your brand. Encourage your followers to use your branded hashtag when sharing content related to your products or services, which can help increase brand awareness and user-generated content.

Don't overdo it: While hashtags are useful, using too many can make your posts look cluttered or spammy. Focus on using 5-10 relevant hashtags that genuinely help your content reach the right audience.

Leverage User-Generated Content (UGC)

User-generated content (UGC) is any content—photos, videos, reviews, or testimonials—created by your customers or followers. UGC is valuable because it serves as social proof, showing potential customers that real people love and use your products or services.

Here's how to leverage UGC:

Encourage your audience to share: Ask your customers to share photos or videos of themselves using your product. You can incentivize this by offering a discount, featuring them on your social media page, or entering them into a giveaway.

Feature UGC on your platforms: When customers tag your business in their posts, share their content on your own social media profiles. This not only builds credibility but also shows appreciation for your community.

Create a hashtag campaign: Encourage your audience to use a specific hashtag when they share content related to your brand. This makes it easier for you to track UGC and engage with your customers. For example, brands like Lululemon use hashtags like #TheSweatLife to encourage users to share their fitness journeys.

Invest in Paid Social Media Advertising

While organic reach is valuable, social media platforms have increasingly become pay-to-play environments. As a solopreneur, you don't need to spend a fortune on ads, but a small investment in paid social media advertising can help you expand your reach and target specific audiences.

Here's how to make the most of paid advertising:

Set a budget: Determine how much you're willing to spend on ads each month. Even a modest budget can generate significant results if you target the right audience and use the right messaging.

Target your audience: Social media platforms like Facebook and Instagram allow you to target ads based on specific demographics, interests, behaviors, and even geographic locations. Use this feature to ensure your ads are reaching the people most likely to engage with your brand.

Test different ads: Experiment with different ad formats, such as carousel ads, video ads, or story ads. Test different messaging, images, and CTAs to see what resonates most with your audience. Monitor the performance of your ads and optimize based on the results.

Retargeting: Retargeting ads show your content to people who have already interacted with your brand, such as visiting your website or engaging with your social media posts. These ads can help you stay top-of-mind with potential customers and encourage them to complete a purchase.

Analyze Your Results and Adjust

To succeed in social media marketing, it's important to continually analyze your results and adjust your strategy accordingly. Use the built-in analytics tools available on each platform to monitor key metrics such as:

Engagement: Track likes, comments, shares, and saves to see which types of content resonate most with your audience.

Reach and impressions: These metrics show how many people have seen your posts and how often your content has appeared in users' feeds.

Follower growth: Keep an eye on how your audience is growing over time. Analyze which posts or campaigns contributed to the largest spikes in follower growth.

Conversions: If your goal is to drive sales, track how many conversions or purchases came from your social media campaigns.

Based on this data, adjust your content strategy, posting frequency, and ad spend to maximize your return on investment.

Social media marketing offers modern solopreneurs an incredible opportunity to build their brand, connect with their audience, and grow their business. By choosing the right platforms, developing a clear strategy, focusing on engagement, and using tools like hashtags, UGC, and paid ads, you can create a powerful social media presence that drives real results. The key to success is consistency, authenticity, and a willingness to experiment with different types of content and strategies. With the right approach, social media marketing can become one of your most effective tools for business growth.

Using YouTube as a Business Growth Tool

YouTube has evolved into one of the most powerful platforms for business growth, especially for solopreneurs looking to reach a global audience, build their personal brand, and showcase their expertise. With over 2 billion monthly active users, YouTube offers solopreneurs an incredible opportunity to create and share valuable video content that can attract potential customers, increase engagement, and establish authority in their niche. What sets YouTube apart from other platforms is its search engine functionality, allowing videos to be discovered long after they've been uploaded, providing consistent traffic and growth opportunities.

Here's how you can effectively use YouTube as a business growth tool and tap into its full potential for your solopreneur venture.

Create a YouTube Channel Aligned with Your Brand

Before you start creating videos, the first step is to set up a YouTube channel that reflects your brand and values. Your channel is the face of your business on YouTube, so it's important to present it in a way that feels professional and inviting to your target audience.

Channel Name: Choose a name that reflects your business or personal brand. If you're a solopreneur using your personal name as the brand, you can use that for your channel. Alternatively, you can use your business name or a catchy name that reflects your niche.

Profile Picture and Banner: Use a professional profile picture (like your logo or headshot) and design an engaging channel banner that conveys your brand message. Make sure the banner clearly communicates what your channel is about, using your tagline, brand colors, or a brief description of your niche.

Channel Description: Write a compelling channel description that explains who you are, what your business is about, and what type of content viewers can expect. Include relevant keywords to help people find your channel through search.

Customize Your Channel Layout: Organize your content by adding sections to your channel homepage. You can feature playlists, popular videos, or specific content categories, making it easier for visitors to navigate your channel and discover your best content.

Develop a Content Strategy

Having a clear content strategy is essential for leveraging YouTube as a business growth tool. Your videos should provide value to your target audience, whether it's through education, entertainment, or inspiration. The key is to create content that aligns with your business goals and addresses the needs and interests of your viewers.

Identify Your Niche: Focus on creating content that aligns with your area of expertise and serves a specific audience. For example, if you're a fitness coach, you could create workout tutorials, nutrition tips, and motivational content. If you're a graphic designer, you might create tutorials on design tools, portfolio reviews, or creative tips.

Solve Problems: One of the most effective ways to grow your channel and attract potential customers is by solving common problems your audience faces. Create how-to videos, tutorials, and guides that address specific pain points or answer frequently asked questions in your niche. For example, a business coach could create videos on productivity hacks, marketing strategies, or time management tips for entrepreneurs.

Leverage Keywords: YouTube is the second-largest search engine in the world, so it's important to optimize your content for search. Conduct keyword research using tools like TubeBuddy, VidIQ, or Google's Keyword Planner to identify terms your audience is searching for. Incorporate these keywords in your video titles, descriptions, and tags to improve discoverability.

Plan Consistent Uploads: Consistency is crucial for building momentum on YouTube. Create a content calendar and commit to uploading videos regularly, whether it's once a week, biweekly, or monthly. Consistent uploads help keep your audience engaged and signal to YouTube's algorithm that your channel is active, increasing your chances of being recommended to new viewers.

Create High-Quality, Engaging Videos

The quality of your videos plays a significant role in keeping viewers engaged and encouraging them to subscribe to your channel. While you don't need a huge budget to create YouTube content, paying attention to certain elements can elevate the overall production value and impact of your videos.

Plan Your Content: Before filming, outline your video content with a clear structure. Have a script or bullet points ready so you stay on track and deliver your message clearly. Avoid rambling or going off-topic, as this can cause viewers to lose interest.

Invest in Good Lighting and Sound: While fancy equipment isn't necessary, investing in good lighting and sound is important. Natural lighting works well, but you can also use affordable ring lights or softboxes to brighten up your videos. For sound, consider using a lapel or USB microphone to ensure clear audio.

Hook Your Viewers Early: The first 10-15 seconds of your video are crucial in capturing attention. Start with an engaging hook that grabs the viewer's interest, such as posing a question, sharing an interesting fact, or previewing what they will learn or gain by watching.

Keep Your Videos Concise: Attention spans are short, so aim to keep your videos concise and to the point. While some topics may require longer videos, try to keep most of your content between 5 and 10 minutes long, especially when starting out. If you have a lot to cover, consider breaking it up into a series of shorter videos.

Add Visuals and Graphics: Use visuals like slides, infographics, or on-screen text to enhance your videos and make them more engaging. You can also edit your videos to include transitions, captions, or callouts that emphasize key points.

Optimize Your Videos for Discoverability

YouTube's search engine plays a major role in driving organic traffic to your videos. To maximize your visibility, you need to optimize your videos for search and discovery. This process is known as YouTube SEO.

Compelling Titles: Write attention-grabbing titles that clearly convey the content of your video while incorporating relevant keywords. The title should be concise (under 60 characters) and give viewers a reason to click. For example, "5 Productivity Hacks for Solopreneurs" is more compelling than "Productivity Tips."

Detailed Descriptions: Your video description provides an opportunity to give more context about your content. Write detailed descriptions that summarize the video, include keywords, and encourage viewers to take action (e.g., subscribe, like, or visit your website). You can also include links to your website, social media profiles, or relevant products or services.

Use Tags: Add relevant tags to help YouTube understand the topic of your video. Use both broad and specific keywords to maximize your chances of being discovered. For example, if your video is about time management, you could use tags like "time management tips," "productivity," "solopreneur hacks," and "how to manage time."

Custom Thumbnails: Thumbnails play a big role in driving clicks. Create custom thumbnails that are visually appealing and clearly represent the content of the video. Use bold text, colors, and images to grab attention and entice viewers to watch. Tools like Canva make it easy to design custom thumbnails, even if you don't have design experience.

End Screens and Cards: Use YouTube's end screens and cards to promote other videos on your channel, encourage viewers to subscribe, or direct them to your website. End screens appear at the end of your videos and can include clickable links to other content, while cards can be added throughout your video to point viewers to relevant resources.

Build an Engaged Audience

Building an engaged audience on YouTube is key to growing your business. The more engaged your viewers are, the more likely they are to subscribe, share your videos, and eventually become customers.

Encourage Subscriptions: At the end of each video, remind viewers to subscribe to your channel. You can also add a "subscribe" graphic or animation in your videos. When people subscribe, they're more likely to return to your channel, increasing your long-term growth.

Engage with Comments: Make it a habit to respond to comments on your videos. Engaging with your audience shows that you value their feedback and encourages more interaction. This helps build a sense of community around your channel.

Ask for Feedback: Encourage your viewers to share their opinions or ask questions in the comments. You can even create videos based on their feedback, showing that you listen to your audience's needs. This interaction strengthens your connection with viewers and makes them feel like part of your journey.

Collaborate with Others: Collaborating with other YouTubers or influencers in your niche can introduce your channel to a broader audience. Look for creators whose audience aligns with yours and explore ways to collaborate, such as guest appearances, joint tutorials, or shout-outs.

Monetize Your YouTube Channel

Once your channel starts gaining traction, you can explore monetization options to turn your YouTube presence into a revenue stream for your business.

Ad Revenue: YouTube allows you to run ads on your videos through the YouTube Partner Program. To qualify, you need at least 1,000 subscribers and 4,000 watch hours over the past 12 months. Ad revenue can provide a passive income stream as your channel grows.

Affiliate Marketing: Promote products or services through affiliate marketing in your videos. You can include affiliate links in your video descriptions, earning commissions on sales generated through those links.

Sell Products or Services: YouTube is an excellent platform to promote your own products or services. Whether it's digital products, physical goods, or consulting services, use your videos to showcase the benefits of what you offer and direct viewers to your website for purchases.

Sponsored Content: As your channel grows, brands may approach you for sponsorship deals. Sponsored content involves promoting a brand's product or service in exchange for payment or free products. Just be sure that any sponsorship aligns with your brand and provides value to your audience.

PROMOTE YOUR YOUTUBE Content across Platforms

While YouTube has its own discovery tools, promoting your videos on other platforms can help drive more traffic to your channel. Share your YouTube videos on your website, blog, email newsletters, and social media profiles. Use snippets or teasers on Instagram, Facebook, and LinkedIn to encourage people to watch the full video on YouTube. Cross-promotion helps maximize your content's reach and introduces your videos to new audiences.

YouTube is a powerful business growth tool for solopreneurs, offering opportunities to build authority, engage with your audience, and attract new customers through video content. By creating valuable, high-quality videos, optimizing them for discoverability, and building an engaged community, you can use YouTube to grow your brand, increase visibility, and generate revenue. With the right strategy, consistency, and creativity, YouTube can become a key pillar in your solopreneur marketing efforts, helping you scale your business in the digital world.

Leveraging Facebook for Solopreneur Success

Facebook remains one of the most effective platforms for solopreneurs to build a business, engage with their audience, and generate sales. With over 2.8 billion active users, Facebook offers solopreneurs access to a broad audience and a suite of tools designed to help grow their business. Whether you're offering products, services, or expertise, Facebook allows you to promote your business, establish credibility, and connect with potential customers in a meaningful way.

To successfully leverage Facebook for your solopreneur venture, it's essential to understand how to use the platform's various features strategically and integrate it into your overall marketing strategy. Here's how you can maximize Facebook's potential for your solopreneur success.

Create a Facebook Business Page

Your first step is to set up a **Facebook Business Page**. Unlike personal profiles, business pages give you access to tools that allow you to track analytics, run ads, and connect with your audience more effectively. A business page also adds credibility, showing that you're serious about your brand.

To create an engaging Facebook Business Page:

Choose a profile picture and cover photo that reflect your brand identity. Your profile picture might be your logo, and your cover photo could showcase your product or service or include a tagline that communicates your mission.

Complete the "About" section with a compelling description of your business, including what you do, who you serve, and the value you offer. This is also the place to include essential information like your website, contact details, and business hours.

Add call-to-action buttons like "Shop Now," "Book Now," or "Contact Us" to guide visitors to take the next step, whether it's purchasing a product or contacting you for a service.

Build Your Audience and Community

Growing an engaged audience is crucial to making Facebook work for your solopreneur business. While gaining likes and followers is important, it's more valuable to focus on building a community that actively engages with your content.

Here's how to build an engaged Facebook community:

Invite your contacts: Start by inviting friends, family, and professional contacts to like your page. If you have an email list, send an invitation encouraging them to follow you on Facebook.

Create valuable content: Consistently share content that resonates with your audience. Whether it's tips, tutorials, behind-the-scenes insights, or news about your business, your content should provide value and spark conversations. Avoid being overly promotional—focus on engaging and informing your audience.

Engage with your audience: Respond to comments, answer questions, and thank people for sharing your content. The more you engage with your followers, the more connected they will feel to your brand.

Use Facebook Groups: Consider creating or joining **Facebook Groups** related to your niche. Groups provide an opportunity to build a more intimate community where members can interact, share advice, and discuss relevant topics. Creating your own group can position you as a leader in your space, while joining established groups can help you network and reach potential customers organically.

Post Consistently and at Optimal Times

Consistency is key when it comes to maintaining an active presence on Facebook. Posting regularly keeps your audience engaged and reminds them of your business. However, quality is just as important as quantity, so aim to share content that is both valuable and relevant to your followers.

Some tips for posting consistently:

Develop a content calendar: Plan your posts in advance by creating a content calendar. This helps you stay organized and ensures you're posting a variety of content types (e.g., educational posts, promotions, user-generated content, and interactive polls).

Post at optimal times: Analyze your page insights to determine when your audience is most active on Facebook. Generally, the best times to post are during weekday mornings or early afternoons, but this can vary depending on your audience. Posting at optimal times increases the likelihood of your content being seen.

Mix up content formats: Keep your feed dynamic by mixing different types of content, such as videos, live streams, photos, text updates, and polls. Video content, in particular, tends to perform well on Facebook, so consider incorporating short videos, tutorials, or live streams into your strategy.

Use Facebook Live to Connect with Your Audience

Facebook Live is a powerful tool for solopreneurs to connect with their audience in real-time, offering a way to engage followers on a more personal level. Live videos have higher engagement rates than pre-recorded content and can help you build trust with your audience.

Here are some ways to leverage Facebook Live:

Host Q&A sessions: Use Facebook Live to answer questions from your audience about your business, products, or industry. This interaction can help position you as an expert and provide real-time value to your followers.

Give behind-the-scenes looks: Show your audience how your business operates behind the scenes. Whether it's a tour of your workspace, a product creation process, or a day in your life as a solopreneur, behind-the-scenes content makes your brand more relatable and human.

Launch new products or services: Use Facebook Live to announce and showcase new products or services. The real-time interaction can create excitement, and you can respond to questions and feedback immediately.

Host live events or workshops: If your business is knowledge-based, consider hosting live workshops, tutorials, or webinars. This provides value to your audience and showcases your expertise.

Run Targeted Facebook Ads

Facebook offers one of the most advanced advertising platforms, allowing solopreneurs to create highly targeted ad campaigns even with a modest budget. Facebook Ads can help you reach a larger audience, generate leads, and increase sales.

To make the most of Facebook advertising:

Define your objective: Before creating an ad, determine what you want to achieve. Facebook Ads Manager allows you to choose from various objectives, such as driving traffic to your website, increasing page engagement, generating leads, or boosting sales.

Target your audience: Facebook's targeting options allow you to reach your ideal customers based on demographics, interests, behaviors, location, and even past interactions with your brand. Use detailed targeting to ensure your ads are seen by people who are most likely to engage with your business.

Use engaging visuals and copy: Create visually appealing ads with strong, clear messaging. High-quality images, videos, or carousel ads with multiple product images tend to perform well. Your ad copy should include a strong call-to-action (CTA) that prompts viewers to take the desired action, such as "Shop Now," "Sign Up," or "Learn More."

Set a budget and monitor performance: Start with a small budget to test different ad variations. Monitor your ad performance through Facebook Ads Manager and optimize based on metrics like click-through rates (CTR), conversions, and engagement. Adjust your targeting or creative based on what's working.

Build and Engage with Facebook Groups

Facebook Groups are an invaluable tool for solopreneurs to create a community around their brand. Unlike Facebook Pages, Groups allow for more direct interaction, collaboration, and discussion among members.

How to leverage Facebook Groups:

Create your own group: Consider creating a group that aligns with your niche or industry. For example, if you're a health coach, you could create a group where members share wellness tips, workout routines, and nutrition advice. This positions you as a thought leader and creates a sense of community around your brand.

Engage actively: Be an active participant in your group by posting regularly, asking questions, responding to comments, and facilitating discussions. The more value you provide, the more engaged your community will be.

Share exclusive content: Offer your group members exclusive content, such as free webinars, discounts, or early access to new products. This can encourage more people to join your group and foster loyalty among your followers.

Use Facebook Insights to Improve Your Strategy

Facebook's built-in analytics tool, **Facebook Insights**, allows you to track your page's performance and analyze the effectiveness of your content and campaigns. Using these insights, you can fine-tune your strategy and improve your overall results.

Key metrics to track:

Engagement: Monitor likes, comments, and shares on your posts to see which types of content resonate most with your audience.

Reach and impressions: Reach measures the number of unique users who have seen your content, while impressions count how many times your content has been displayed. This helps you understand how far your content is spreading.

Clicks and website visits: If your goal is to drive traffic to your website, track the number of clicks your posts or ads generate. Insights can also show which specific posts drive the most traffic.

Audience demographics: Facebook Insights provides data about your audience, including their age, gender, location, and interests. Use this data to tailor your content and ads to better align with your audience's preferences.

Leverage Facebook Messenger for Customer Service

Facebook Messenger can be an excellent tool for providing customer service and building stronger relationships with your customers. Many consumers prefer communicating with businesses through messaging, as it's quick, convenient, and personal.

Here's how to use Messenger effectively:

Set up automated responses: You can set up automated responses for frequently asked questions or for welcoming new customers. This ensures that you're providing quick answers even if you're not available to respond immediately.

Use Messenger for lead generation: Messenger is also a great way to generate leads by offering personalized conversations. For example, you can run Facebook ads with a "Message Us" CTA, allowing potential customers to directly inquire about your products or services.

Follow up with customers: Messenger allows you to build a more personal relationship with your audience by following up with customers after purchases or interactions. This can help improve customer retention and encourage repeat business.

Facebook offers solopreneurs an incredible range of tools and features that can help grow a business, build community, and generate sales. By creating a professional Facebook Business Page, engaging with your audience, leveraging Facebook Ads, and actively using tools like Facebook Groups and Messenger, you can establish a strong presence on the platform and connect with your target audience in meaningful ways.

The key to success on Facebook is consistency, engagement, and providing value to your audience. By sharing quality content, responding to comments, and using insights to refine your strategy, you can harness the full potential of Facebook to build a thriving solopreneur business.

How to Tap into Instagram for Your Business

Instagram has become a go-to platform for solopreneurs to promote their businesses, build brands, and engage with potential customers. With its highly visual nature and diverse audience, Instagram offers solopreneurs an ideal space to showcase products or services, connect with followers, and foster a community. Leveraging Instagram for your business can help drive traffic, generate leads, and build brand loyalty, all while providing a creative outlet for sharing your story. Here's how to tap into Instagram to grow your business as a solopreneur.

Set Up an Instagram Business Account

The first step to using Instagram for business is setting up a **Business Account**. Unlike personal profiles, a business account provides access to analytics, advertising tools, and other features that help you track performance and optimize your strategy.

To set up your Instagram Business Account:

Switch to a business account: If you already have a personal Instagram account, you can easily switch it to a business account in your settings. If not, you can create a new business account from scratch.

Complete your profile: Choose a username that matches your brand name, and use a high-quality logo or photo as your profile picture. Write a concise, compelling bio that explains who you are, what you offer, and why people should follow you. Include a link to your website, online store, or other key landing page.

Add contact options: Instagram Business Accounts allow you to include contact buttons (email, phone, or directions) so that potential customers can easily reach you.

Define Your Instagram Goals

Before diving into content creation, it's essential to define clear goals for your Instagram strategy. What do you hope to achieve? Setting specific goals helps you stay focused and measure your success.

Here are a few common Instagram goals for solopreneurs:

Increase brand awareness: Use Instagram to introduce your business to a larger audience and showcase what makes your brand unique.

Generate leads and sales: Drive traffic to your website, product pages, or online store by using Instagram to showcase your offerings and encourage conversions.

Build community: Engage with your followers by creating a sense of community around your brand. This can involve fostering conversations, sharing user-generated content, and interacting regularly with your audience.

Grow your following: Attract more followers by creating valuable content, using strategic hashtags, and engaging with other accounts in your niche.

Create Engaging, On-Brand Content

Instagram is a visual platform, and creating high-quality, on-brand content is crucial for attracting and retaining followers. Your content should align with your business's aesthetics, tone, and messaging while also resonating with your target audience.

Here's how to create engaging content that supports your business goals:

Visual consistency: Establish a cohesive visual style for your Instagram feed by using consistent colors, fonts, and filters. This creates a recognizable brand identity that helps your account stand out. Use design tools like Canva to create graphics, posts, and stories that match your brand's aesthetic.

High-quality images and videos: Invest in creating high-quality visuals that showcase your products or services. Use natural lighting, clean backgrounds, and clear focus to ensure your content looks professional. You don't need to be a professional photographer—modern smartphones have excellent cameras that can produce great results with the right composition and lighting.

Mix content types: Keep your feed dynamic by mixing up different types of content. Share product photos, behind-the-scenes footage, user-generated content, tutorials, testimonials, and lifestyle shots. Don't be afraid to experiment with different formats like carousel posts, videos, Reels, and Instagram Stories.

Tell a story: Storytelling is an effective way to engage your audience emotionally. Use captions to share your business journey, talk about challenges you've overcome, or explain the inspiration behind your products. Authenticity resonates with audiences, so let your personality and mission shine through.

Use Instagram Reels: Reels, which are short, entertaining videos, are a great way to increase your visibility on Instagram. They tend to get more reach than regular posts because Instagram prioritizes Reels in its algorithm. Use Reels to showcase product features, share tutorials, or create fun, engaging content that captures attention quickly.

Leverage Instagram Stories

Instagram Stories are a powerful tool for solopreneurs to engage with their audience in real-time. Stories disappear after 24 hours, making them perfect for sharing quick updates, promotions, or behind-the-scenes moments.

Here's how to use Instagram Stories effectively:

Show the human side of your brand: Use Stories to share informal, behind-the-scenes content that gives your audience a glimpse into your day-to-day operations. Whether it's packaging orders, working on a new project, or answering questions, Stories help make your brand more relatable and authentic.

Use interactive features: Instagram Stories come with built-in features like polls, question boxes, and quizzes that encourage audience interaction. Use these tools to engage with your followers, gather feedback, or spark conversations. You can even run contests or giveaways through Stories to boost engagement.

Highlight important content: Since Stories disappear after 24 hours, you can save your best Stories to **Story Highlights** on your profile. Use highlights to showcase categories like products, testimonials, FAQs, or events. Story Highlights serve as a curated collection of your best content for new visitors to explore.

Use Hashtags Strategically

Hashtags are one of the best ways to increase the discoverability of your posts and attract new followers. By using relevant hashtags, you can reach users who are interested in the topics or products you're posting about, even if they're not already following you.

To use hashtags effectively:

Research popular hashtags: Identify hashtags that are commonly used in your niche. You can use tools like Hashtagify or simply explore Instagram to see what hashtags influencers and competitors are using. Choose a mix of popular and niche-specific hashtags.

Use branded hashtags: Create a unique hashtag for your business, such as your brand name or slogan, and encourage your followers to use it when posting about your products. This builds a sense of community and helps you gather user-generated content.

Don't overdo it: Instagram allows up to 30 hashtags per post, but using too many can make your post look cluttered. Aim for around 5 to 10 highly relevant hashtags that will help your content get discovered by the right audience.

Engage with Your Audience

Building an engaged community on Instagram goes beyond simply posting content. Interaction is key. Responding to comments, liking other people's posts, and building relationships with your followers helps foster loyalty and connection.

HERE'S HOW TO ENGAGE meaningfully with your audience:

Respond to comments and messages: Make it a habit to reply to comments on your posts and direct messages. When followers see that you take the time to interact, they're more likely to continue engaging with your content.

Follow relevant accounts: Engage with other businesses, influencers, or solopreneurs in your niche. Leave thoughtful comments on their posts, share relevant content, and build relationships that can lead to collaborations, partnerships, or a larger following.

Ask questions: Encourage interaction by asking questions in your posts or Stories. For example, if you're launching a new product, ask your followers for their input or feedback. This invites conversation and helps your audience feel more connected to your brand.

Use Instagram Polls and Questions: Use the poll or question features in Instagram Stories to ask your followers their opinions, preferences, or feedback on topics related to your business. This encourages engagement and gives you valuable insights into what your audience wants.

Partner with Influencers and Collaborators

Collaborating with influencers or other solopreneurs can help you reach a larger audience and gain credibility. Influencer marketing on Instagram has proven to be highly effective, especially for brands looking to build awareness and trust.

Here's how to approach collaborations:

Choose the right influencers: Look for influencers whose values align with your brand and who have an engaged following that matches your target audience. Micro-influencers, those with smaller but highly engaged audiences, are often a good fit for solopreneurs because they tend to be more affordable and approachable.

Offer value: Whether it's a product exchange, a paid partnership, or a shout-out, make sure both parties benefit from the collaboration. Be clear about what you want to achieve, such as increasing followers, driving sales, or creating brand awareness.

Collaborate with other solopreneurs: Don't limit your collaborations to influencers. Partner with other solopreneurs in complementary niches to create content together, run joint giveaways, or cross-promote each other's products.

Utilize Instagram Ads

While organic growth is important, Instagram Ads allow you to reach a broader audience and drive targeted traffic to your business. Instagram's advertising tools allow you to target specific demographics, interests, and behaviors, ensuring your ads are seen by people who are most likely to be interested in your products or services.

To get the most out of Instagram Ads:

Set a clear objective: Whether your goal is to increase brand awareness, drive traffic to your website, or generate sales, be clear about your objective before setting up an ad campaign.

Use engaging visuals: High-quality visuals are essential for Instagram Ads. Use eye-catching images or videos that align with your brand and include a clear call-to-action (CTA) like "Shop Now," "Learn More," or "Sign Up."

Test different ad formats: Experiment with different types of ads, such as photo ads, video ads, carousel ads (multiple images), or Story ads. Monitor performance to see which format drives the most engagement or conversions.

Target your audience: Instagram's ad platform allows you to target your ads based on factors like location, age, gender, interests, and behaviors. You can also create lookalike audiences to target users who are similar to your existing followers or customers.

Analyze and Adjust with Instagram Insights

Instagram Business Accounts provide access to **Instagram Insights**, a built-in analytics tool that helps you track the performance of your posts, Stories, and audience engagement. By regularly reviewing these metrics, you can optimize your strategy for better results.

Key metrics to track:

Engagement rate: Monitor likes, comments, shares, and saves to see which types of posts resonate most with your audience.

Follower demographics: Learn about the age, gender, location, and active hours of your followers to tailor your content more effectively.

Reach and impressions: Track how many people are seeing your posts (reach) and how often they're being shown (impressions). This helps you understand the overall visibility of your content.

Website clicks and conversions: If you're driving traffic to your website, track how many clicks your posts, Stories, or ads generate. You can also use tracking tools like Google Analytics to measure conversions from Instagram. By analyzing your results, you can identify which content performs best, which times of day your audience is most active, and what strategies are helping you grow your business.

Instagram is a powerful platform for solopreneurs to grow their business, connect with their audience, and build a strong brand presence. By creating high-quality, engaging content, using hashtags strategically, and interacting with your followers regularly, you can increase your visibility and foster a loyal community. Leverage tools like Instagram Stories, Reels, and Ads to further amplify your reach and drive traffic to your website or store. With consistency, creativity, and an authentic approach, Instagram can become a key part of your solopreneur success.

Exploring LinkedIn for Solopreneur Opportunities

LinkedIn is a powerful platform for solopreneurs looking to build professional networks, find clients, and establish themselves as industry experts. While LinkedIn is often thought of as a platform for corporate professionals and job seekers, it offers solopreneurs valuable opportunities to connect with potential clients, collaborators, and mentors. By leveraging LinkedIn strategically, you can tap into its professional audience, generate leads, and grow your business.

Here's how you can explore LinkedIn for solopreneur opportunities and make the most of its features to expand your network and business.

Optimize Your LinkedIn Profile for Your Business

Your LinkedIn profile is essentially your digital resume and storefront, and it needs to reflect your personal brand and business. A well-optimized profile builds credibility and helps you make a strong first impression with potential clients or partners.

Here's how to optimize your LinkedIn profile for solopreneur success:

Profile picture and cover photo: Use a high-quality, professional headshot as your profile picture. For your cover photo, consider an image that represents your brand or highlights your services. It could be your logo, a slogan, or an image that speaks to your business.

Headline: Your headline should be more than just your job title. It's one of the first things people see, so make it clear what you do and how you help people. For example, instead of "Freelance Graphic Designer," try "Helping businesses create stunning visual identities that stand out."

About section: Write a compelling summary that tells your story as a solopreneur. Highlight your expertise, the problems you solve, and the value you bring to clients. Keep it focused on how you can help others, and include relevant keywords that reflect your industry to improve searchability.

Experience and services: List your experience, but emphasize the services you offer as a solopreneur. Be specific about the type of work you do, your target audience, and the results you've achieved for clients. Use bullet points to clearly outline the key services you provide.

Skills and endorsements: Add relevant skills that showcase your expertise, and request endorsements from clients or colleagues. These endorsements add social proof and increase your credibility on the platform.

Recommendations: Ask satisfied clients or collaborators for recommendations. These act as testimonials and give potential clients more confidence in your abilities.

BUILD AND EXPAND YOUR Network

Building a strong LinkedIn network is key to unlocking opportunities as a solopreneur. The larger and more relevant your network, the more likely you are to connect with potential clients, partners, and collaborators.

Here's how to grow your LinkedIn network:

Connect with people in your industry: Start by connecting with people you've worked with in the past, industry peers, and potential clients. Personalize your connection requests with a brief message explaining why you'd like to connect, especially if you're reaching out to someone you haven't met before.

Engage with your connections: Networking on LinkedIn isn't just about connecting with people—it's about building relationships. Engage with your connections by liking, commenting on, and sharing their posts. This helps you stay visible and positions you as an active participant in your industry.

Join relevant LinkedIn Groups: LinkedIn Groups are a great way to connect with professionals in your niche, exchange ideas, and promote your expertise. Join groups where your target audience or industry peers are active. Share insights, participate in discussions, and offer valuable advice. Avoid being overly promotional, as LinkedIn Groups are primarily for networking and learning.

Attend virtual events: LinkedIn frequently hosts virtual networking events, webinars, and industry-related discussions. Participating in these events is an excellent way to meet new people, gain insights, and expand your network.

Share Valuable Content Regularly

Positioning yourself as an expert in your field is essential for solopreneur success, and LinkedIn provides a platform for you to share your knowledge and insights. Posting valuable content regularly not only builds your personal brand but also attracts potential clients and collaborators.

Here's how to create and share content that boosts your credibility:

Write thought leadership articles: LinkedIn's publishing platform allows you to write long-form articles on topics related to your industry. Writing thought leadership content showcases your expertise, generates engagement, and can be shared within your network and beyond. Use these articles to address industry trends, share tips, or provide solutions to common problems your audience faces.

Share short posts: In addition to articles, share shorter posts regularly. These can include quick tips, reflections on your solopreneur journey, industry news, or insights from recent projects. Consistently sharing content helps keep you visible to your network and provides value to your followers.

Repurpose existing content: If you have a blog or YouTube channel, repurpose that content for LinkedIn. Share snippets, summaries, or highlights from your other platforms to engage your LinkedIn audience. Include links back to your website or other platforms to drive traffic.

Use multimedia content: Incorporate images, infographics, and videos into your LinkedIn posts. Multimedia content is more engaging and can help you stand out in the news feed. For example, if you're a designer, share samples of your work or client testimonials in a visually appealing format.

Share client success stories: Highlighting successful client projects or case studies is a great way to demonstrate the value of your services. Share how you helped a client solve a problem or achieve a specific goal, and provide tangible results that showcase your impact.

Engage in Meaningful Conversations

Active engagement on LinkedIn is critical to building relationships and expanding your influence. Don't just post and disappear—participate in conversations, respond to comments, and engage with others in your industry.

Here's how to engage meaningfully:

Comment on others' posts: Be thoughtful when commenting on other people's posts. Share your insights, ask questions, or offer encouragement. This builds relationships and increases your visibility within your industry.

Respond to comments on your posts: When people comment on your posts, make sure to reply and engage with them. This keeps the conversation going and signals to others that you value interaction.

Message connections: Use LinkedIn's messaging feature to follow up with new connections, nurture relationships, or explore collaboration opportunities. Personalize your messages rather than using generic templates, and focus on building a genuine connection before pitching any services.

Use LinkedIn's Lead Generation Tools

For solopreneurs, LinkedIn is a valuable tool for generating leads and finding clients. Whether you're offering consulting services, selling products, or promoting freelance work, LinkedIn offers features designed to help you identify and connect with potential clients.

Here's how to tap into LinkedIn's lead generation features:

LinkedIn Sales Navigator: This premium tool allows you to filter your search for leads by industry, location, job title, and more. It's especially useful if you're targeting a specific type of client or looking to generate leads in a particular sector. Sales Navigator also provides insights into your prospects and their activities, helping you craft more personalized outreach messages.

Advanced search filters: Even without Sales Navigator, LinkedIn's search feature allows you to use advanced filters to find potential clients or collaborators. You can search by keywords, location, company size, and job title to identify the right people to connect with.

LinkedIn InMail: If you're using a premium LinkedIn account, you have access to **InMail**, which allows you to send direct messages to people outside your network. InMail can be a powerful tool for reaching potential clients with personalized messages. Make sure to craft your messages carefully, focusing on how you can provide value to the recipient.

LinkedIn Ads: If you have a marketing budget, LinkedIn Ads can help you reach a highly targeted audience. You can create ads that promote your services, drive traffic to your website, or encourage users to download a lead magnet. LinkedIn's precise targeting options allow you to reach decision-makers and professionals who are most likely to be interested in your offerings.

Showcase Your Expertise with LinkedIn's Features

LinkedIn offers various features that solopreneurs can use to highlight their expertise and stand out from the crowd.

LinkedIn Showcase Pages: If you offer different services or target multiple audiences, consider creating **Showcase Pages**. These are extensions of your LinkedIn Business Page and allow you to focus on a particular aspect of your business. Each Showcase Page can have its own content, followers, and updates, which helps you segment your marketing efforts.

LinkedIn Events: Hosting or attending LinkedIn Events is a great way to network and showcase your expertise. You can organize virtual events like webinars, workshops, or Q&A sessions related to your industry. Promoting these events through LinkedIn allows you to engage with your network and attract new leads.

LinkedIn Live: Similar to other live streaming platforms, **LinkedIn Live** lets you broadcast real-time video content to your network. Use LinkedIn Live to host discussions, share insights, or provide tutorials. It's an excellent way to build rapport and engage with your audience in a more personal format.

Build Your Personal Brand and Credibility

As a solopreneur, your personal brand is often synonymous with your business. Building your personal brand on LinkedIn not only helps you attract clients but also positions you as a thought leader in your industry.

Here's how to strengthen your personal brand on LinkedIn:

Be consistent: Consistency is key when building a personal brand. Make sure your posts, comments, and interactions align with your brand values, tone, and messaging. Over time, this consistency will help establish you as a reliable and credible figure in your niche.

Showcase your accomplishments: Don't be afraid to share your wins, whether it's a successful client project, a new certification, or a speaking engagement. Highlighting your accomplishments builds credibility and shows potential clients that you're capable of delivering results.

Provide value to your network: Focus on giving more than you take. Share useful content, offer advice, and provide support to your network. The more value you provide, the more people will view you as an expert and be inclined to work with you.

LinkedIn is a powerful platform for solopreneurs to grow their business, build professional networks, and establish authority in their industry. By optimizing your profile, sharing valuable content, engaging with others, and using LinkedIn's lead generation tools, you can tap into countless opportunities for collaboration and client acquisition. With a consistent, strategic approach, LinkedIn can become an essential part of your solopreneur marketing and business development strategy.

Building a Strong Website for Your Solopreneur Business

Building a strong website is essential for solopreneurs looking to establish an online presence, attract clients, and grow their business. Your website serves as a digital storefront and a hub for all your business activities. It's often the first impression potential customers have of your brand, so it's important to create a website that is not only visually appealing but also functional, user-friendly, and optimized for conversions.

Here's a comprehensive guide on how to build a strong website for your solopreneur business:

Choose the Right Website Platform

Selecting the right platform is the foundation of building your website. There are numerous website builders available, each with its own strengths, depending on your needs and technical expertise.

Here are some of the most popular website platforms for solopreneurs:

WordPress: One of the most versatile and widely used platforms, WordPress offers endless customization options. It's great for solopreneurs who want full control over their website's design, functionality, and SEO. While it requires some technical know-how, you can use pre-designed themes and plugins to simplify the process.

Wix: A beginner-friendly website builder with drag-and-drop functionality, Wix is ideal for solopreneurs who want a quick and easy way to build a website. It's especially suited for those who don't have much technical experience but want a polished, professional-looking site.

Squarespace: Known for its beautiful templates and design flexibility, Squarespace is another good option for solopreneurs who prioritize design and aesthetics. It's perfect for creative professionals or anyone looking to showcase a portfolio.

Shopify: If you're a solopreneur with an e-commerce business, Shopify is an excellent choice. It's specifically designed for online stores and comes with built-in features for payment processing, inventory management, and sales analytics.

Weebly: Another user-friendly option, Weebly offers simple drag-and-drop tools for building a website. It's a good choice for solopreneurs who need a basic website without a steep learning curve.

Define Your Website's Purpose and Goals

Before you start building your website, it's important to define its purpose and the specific goals you want to achieve. Knowing the primary objective of your website will help guide its design, content, and overall structure.

COMMON GOALS FOR SOLOPRENEUR websites include:

Building brand awareness: Your website is a platform to showcase your brand's story, values, and offerings. Use it to introduce your business and create a memorable brand presence.

Generating leads: If you're offering services, your website should focus on converting visitors into leads. This may involve having clear call-to-action buttons (CTAs) like "Contact Us," "Book a Consultation," or "Get a Quote."

Driving sales: If you sell products or services online, your website's primary goal is to drive sales. An easy-to-navigate store with clear product descriptions and secure payment processing is essential.

Showcasing expertise: If you're in a knowledge-based industry like consulting or coaching, your website can serve as a platform to showcase your expertise through blog posts, case studies, testimonials, and portfolios.

Once you've identified your website's purpose, design the user experience to lead visitors toward that goal.

Design for User Experience (UX)

A well-designed website should be easy to navigate, visually appealing, and optimized for conversions. The user experience (UX) plays a major role in how potential clients perceive your brand and how likely they are to take action on your site.

Key elements of good UX design include:

Simple navigation: Make it easy for visitors to find what they're looking for by organizing your website into clear, logical sections. Include a top menu with links to important pages, such as "Home," "About," "Services," "Portfolio," and "Contact." Avoid cluttering your site with too many pages or complicated menus.

Mobile responsiveness: Ensure your website looks great and functions properly on all devices, especially mobile phones. More people are browsing the web on their phones, and a mobile-friendly website is crucial for retaining visitors.

Fast loading times: A slow-loading website can drive visitors away. Use optimized images, clean code, and a reliable web hosting service to ensure fast load times.

Clear CTAs: Every page on your website should have a clear call to action that guides visitors toward your goal. Whether it's scheduling a call, signing up for a newsletter, or purchasing a product, make your CTAs prominent and easy to follow.

Clean design: Less is often more when it comes to website design. Stick to a clean, minimalist aesthetic with plenty of white space to ensure your content is easy to read and doesn't overwhelm visitors.

Write Compelling Copy

Your website's copy plays a crucial role in communicating your brand's message, engaging your audience, and driving conversions. Clear, concise, and compelling copy can turn casual visitors into leads or customers.

Here's how to write effective website copy:

Focus on benefits, not just features: When describing your products or services, highlight how they benefit your target audience. For example, rather than just listing features, explain how your service solves a specific problem or improves the user's life.

Speak to your audience: Tailor your language to resonate with your ideal customer. Use a tone and style that reflects your brand's personality, whether that's professional, conversational, or creative.

Be clear and direct: Avoid jargon or complex language. Make your message easy to understand, especially when explaining what your business does and how customers can benefit from it.

Include testimonials or case studies: Social proof is a powerful tool for building trust. Include client testimonials, success stories, or case studies to showcase the impact of your products or services.

Use CTAs strategically: Encourage visitors to take action with strong, persuasive calls to action. Phrases like "Get Started," "Sign Up Now," or "Request a Free Consultation" create urgency and guide visitors toward your goal.

Optimize for SEO

Search engine optimization (SEO) is the process of improving your website's visibility on search engines like Google. Optimizing your website for SEO can help attract organic traffic, meaning potential clients will find you through search results.

To optimize your website for SEO:

Use relevant keywords: Research the keywords your target audience is searching for and incorporate them into your website's content, including page titles, meta descriptions, headers, and body copy.

Optimize your images: Use descriptive file names and alt text for all images on your website. This helps search engines understand what the images are about and can improve your website's SEO.

Improve page speed: As mentioned earlier, fast-loading websites rank better on search engines. Tools like Google PageSpeed Insights can help you identify and fix issues that slow down your site.

Create quality content: Regularly updating your website with high-quality content like blog posts, guides, or case studies can improve your SEO ranking. This content can also position you as an expert in your field and attract more visitors.

Build backlinks: Backlinks from other reputable websites can boost your site's authority and improve your search rankings. You can build backlinks by guest blogging, partnering with other businesses, or getting your content featured on industry websites.

Add Essential Pages

Certain pages are essential to building a strong solopreneur website. These pages help explain who you are, what you offer, and how visitors can engage with your business.

Here are the key pages to include:

Home Page: Your home page is often the first thing visitors see, so it should provide a clear overview of your business. Include a brief introduction, your main services or products, and a strong call to action.

About Page: This page tells the story of your business and helps visitors connect with you on a personal level. Share your background, mission, and values, and explain why your business is the right choice for your target audience.

Services or Products Page: Clearly outline the services or products you offer. Include details like pricing (if applicable), features, benefits, and testimonials to help visitors understand what you provide and why it's valuable.

Portfolio or Case Studies: If you offer creative or professional services, showcase examples of your work through a portfolio or case studies. Highlight successful projects and the results you've achieved for clients.

Blog (optional): A blog is an excellent way to drive traffic to your website, improve SEO, and showcase your expertise. You can write about industry trends, provide helpful tips, or share personal stories related to your solopreneur journey.

Contact Page: Make it easy for potential clients or customers to get in touch with you. Include a simple contact form, your email address, and any other relevant contact information. You can also include links to your social media profiles.

Integrate E-Commerce (If Relevant)

If you're selling products or services directly through your website, you'll need to set up e-commerce functionality. This allows visitors to browse your offerings, add items to a shopping cart, and make purchases directly on your site.

Key elements of e-commerce integration include:

Product pages: Create detailed product pages that include high-quality images, product descriptions, pricing, and specifications. Make sure the checkout process is user-friendly and secure.

Payment gateways: Set up secure payment processing through providers like PayPal, Stripe, or Shopify Payments. Offer multiple payment options to accommodate different customers.

Inventory management: If you're selling physical products, ensure that your website is connected to an inventory management system to keep track of stock levels.

Shipping and returns: Clearly communicate your shipping and return policies to build trust with customers. Make sure these policies are easy to find on your website.

Track and Measure Performance

Once your website is up and running, it's essential to track its performance and make improvements based on data. Use analytics tools like Google Analytics to monitor your website's traffic, user behavior, and conversion rates.

Key metrics to track include:

Traffic sources: Understand where your website visitors are coming from (e.g., organic search, social media, direct traffic) so you can focus your marketing efforts on the most effective channels.

Bounce rate: The bounce rate indicates how many visitors leave your website after viewing just one page. A high bounce rate could suggest issues with your website's design or content.

Conversion rate: Track how many visitors take the desired action on your site, whether it's filling out a contact form, signing up for a newsletter, or making a purchase. If your conversion rate is low, you may need to optimize your CTAs, user experience, or copy.

User behavior: Use tools like heat maps to analyze how users interact with your website. This can help you identify which areas of your site are working well and which need improvement.

Building a strong website is one of the most important steps for solopreneurs to establish credibility, attract clients, and grow their business. By choosing the right platform, designing for user experience, optimizing for SEO, and tracking performance, you can create a website that not only looks professional but also drives real results. A well-designed, functional website acts as a hub for your solopreneur business, helping you connect with your audience, showcase your expertise, and turn visitors into customers.

How to Use Content Marketing to Drive Sales

Content marketing is one of the most effective strategies for solopreneurs to build brand awareness, establish authority, and drive sales. It's a long-term strategy that focuses on creating valuable, relevant, and consistent content to attract and engage your target audience. Unlike traditional marketing, content marketing doesn't rely on hard sales tactics; instead, it aims to educate, entertain, and inspire potential customers, ultimately leading them to purchase your products or services.

Here's how you can use content marketing to drive sales for your solopreneur business:

Understand Your Audience

The foundation of any successful content marketing strategy is a deep understanding of your target audience. You need to know their needs, pain points, preferences, and challenges in order to create content that resonates with them and provides solutions.

To understand your audience:

Create buyer personas: A buyer persona is a semi-fictional representation of your ideal customer. It should include details like their age, profession, income level, interests, and problems they're looking to solve. The more specific you are, the easier it will be to create content that appeals to them.

Conduct audience research: Use tools like Google Analytics, social media insights, and surveys to gather data on your current audience. What kind of content do they engage with most? What questions are they asking? This information can guide your content creation efforts.

Engage with your audience: Regularly interact with your followers on social media, respond to comments, and ask for feedback. This helps you stay in tune with their needs and adapt your content to better serve them.

Understanding your audience ensures that your content marketing strategy is aligned with their goals and provides value, which is essential for driving sales.

Set Clear Content Marketing Goals

Before creating any content, define clear goals for your content marketing strategy. These goals will guide your content creation process and help you measure the effectiveness of your efforts.

Common content marketing goals include:

Increasing brand awareness: Content that educates or entertains can help introduce your brand to a wider audience and build trust over time.

Generating leads: Content like blog posts, eBooks, webinars, or lead magnets can be used to collect email addresses or other contact information from potential customers.

Driving traffic: High-quality content that ranks well in search engines or gets shared on social media can drive traffic to your website, where you can convert visitors into leads or customers.

Increasing sales: Content can help guide potential customers through the buyer's journey by addressing their concerns, providing valuable information, and positioning your product or service as the solution.

By setting specific, measurable goals, you can create content that moves your audience through the sales funnel and ultimately leads to conversions.

Create a Content Strategy Aligned with the Buyer's Journey

The buyer's journey consists of three main stages: **Awareness**, **Consideration**, and **Decision**. Your content should be designed to meet your audience's needs at each stage of the journey and guide them toward making a purchase.

Here's how to create content for each stage:

Awareness Stage: At this stage, potential customers are just becoming aware of their problem or need. Your goal is to create content that educates and raises awareness. This could include blog posts, social media content, infographics, or videos that introduce topics relevant to your business.

Example: If you sell eco-friendly skincare products, you might create a blog post titled "The Top 5 Benefits of Switching to Natural Skincare Products."

Consideration Stage: In the consideration stage, potential customers are evaluating their options and researching solutions. Create content that helps them understand why your product or service is the best choice. This could include detailed product comparisons, case studies, testimonials, webinars, or white papers.

Example: Create a comparison guide showing how your eco-friendly skincare products differ from conventional skincare brands.

Decision Stage: At this stage, the potential customer is ready to make a purchase. Content at this stage should provide clear information about your product or service, as well as how to buy. Use landing pages, product demonstrations, FAQs, and clear calls-to-action to encourage conversions.

Example: Offer a limited-time discount or free shipping for first-time customers who purchase from your website.

By aligning your content with the buyer's journey, you can nurture potential customers through each stage and increase the likelihood of conversion.

CREATE VALUABLE AND Engaging Content

The key to successful content marketing is consistently creating high-quality, valuable content that resonates with your audience. Your content should address their pain points, answer their questions, and provide actionable insights.

Here are some types of content that drive sales:

Blog posts: Blogging is a cornerstone of content marketing. Well-written, informative blog posts can establish you as an expert in your industry and help with SEO, driving organic traffic to your website. For example, if you're a fitness coach, you could write blog posts about workout routines, nutrition tips, or mental wellness.

Videos: Video content is highly engaging and can be used to showcase your products or services, share customer testimonials, or provide tutorials. Platforms like YouTube, Instagram, and TikTok are great for video marketing. A solopreneur selling handmade crafts, for instance, could create "how it's made" videos to show the craftsmanship behind their products.

Lead magnets: Offer free, downloadable resources like eBooks, checklists, or templates in exchange for email addresses. These lead magnets provide value to your audience and help you build a list of qualified leads. For example, a business coach could offer a free PDF guide on "10 Strategies to Boost Your Productivity."

Case studies: Case studies demonstrate how your product or service has helped real customers solve a problem or achieve a goal. They are particularly effective in the consideration and decision stages of the buyer's journey.

Webinars and workshops: Hosting a live webinar or workshop can help you connect with your audience on a deeper level, answer their questions in real time, and demonstrate your expertise. This is an excellent way to build trust and provide value before asking for the sale.

Optimize Your Content for SEO

Search engine optimization (SEO) is critical for ensuring that your content is discoverable by potential customers. Optimizing your content for relevant keywords can help you rank higher in search engine results, driving organic traffic to your website.

Here's how to optimize your content for SEO:

Keyword research: Identify the keywords and phrases your target audience is searching for. Tools like Google Keyword Planner, Ahrefs, and SEMrush can help you find high-volume, low-competition keywords relevant to your industry.

Use keywords strategically: Incorporate your target keywords naturally into your content, including in the title, headers, meta descriptions, and throughout the body of the text. Avoid keyword stuffing, as this can harm your SEO ranking.

Create in-depth content: Long-form content (1,500+ words) tends to rank better on search engines because it provides more comprehensive information. When writing blog posts or articles, aim to provide in-depth answers to your audience's questions.

Optimize images and videos: Ensure that your images and videos are optimized for SEO by using descriptive file names and alt text that includes relevant keywords. This helps search engines understand what the media is about and can improve your chances of appearing in image and video search results.

Internal and external links: Include internal links to other relevant content on your website and external links to authoritative sources. Internal linking helps guide visitors to additional valuable content on your site, while external links improve credibility and SEO rankings.

Mobile optimization: With more users browsing from mobile devices, it's essential that your content is mobile-friendly. Make sure your website and blog posts load quickly, have readable fonts, and are easy to navigate on smartphones and tablets.

By optimizing your content for search engines, you can increase visibility, attract organic traffic, and drive more potential customers to your site.

Promote Your Content

Creating great content is only part of the equation—promoting it is equally important. The more people who see your content, the more opportunities you have to drive traffic and sales.

Here are effective ways to promote your content:

Social media: Share your content on platforms where your audience is active, such as Instagram, Facebook, Twitter, and LinkedIn. Tailor your posts to fit the style of each platform, using images, videos, and engaging captions. Use relevant hashtags to increase discoverability.

Email marketing: Use your email list to distribute content directly to your audience. Regular newsletters with links to your latest blog posts, videos, or guides can help nurture leads and keep your audience engaged with your brand. Include strong calls-to-action that drive readers back to your website.

Collaborate with influencers: Partnering with influencers or thought leaders in your industry can help amplify your content's reach. Influencers can share your content with their audience, helping you tap into a new pool of potential customers.

Guest blogging: Write guest posts for popular blogs or websites in your niche. This not only positions you as an expert in your field but also provides backlinks to your site, improving SEO and driving referral traffic.

Paid promotion: If you have the budget, consider using paid advertising to promote your content. Facebook Ads, Google Ads, and LinkedIn Ads allow you to target specific demographics, ensuring your content reaches the right people. You can promote blog posts, lead magnets, or product pages to drive traffic and conversions.

By strategically promoting your content across multiple channels, you can extend your reach, attract more visitors to your website, and drive higher engagement with your brand.

Use Content to Nurture Leads

Content marketing isn't just about attracting new visitors; it's also about nurturing leads and guiding them through the sales funnel. By consistently delivering valuable content, you can build trust with potential customers and encourage them to take the next step.

Here's how to nurture leads with content:

Email drip campaigns: Set up automated email sequences that deliver content over time to nurture leads. For example, after someone downloads a lead magnet, send a series of follow-up emails with additional resources, blog posts, or special offers. These emails should build a relationship with the prospect and gradually lead them toward making a purchase.

Retargeting ads: Use retargeting ads to reach people who have engaged with your content but haven't yet made a purchase. These ads can remind them about your product or service and encourage them to return to your website to complete their transaction.

Case studies and testimonials: Sharing customer success stories and testimonials in follow-up emails or retargeting ads can help build credibility and trust. People are more likely to convert when they see how others have benefited from your product or service.

Content upgrades: Offer additional resources or premium content to people who have already consumed your free content. For example, if someone reads a blog post, offer them a related eBook or guide in exchange for their email address. This helps move them further down the sales funnel.

By nurturing leads with valuable content, you can build stronger relationships and increase the likelihood of conversion.

Track and Measure Your Results

To ensure your content marketing efforts are driving sales, it's essential to track your results and adjust your strategy based on the data. Regularly reviewing your metrics allows you to see what's working, what's not, and where you can improve.

Key metrics to track include:

Traffic: Monitor the amount of traffic each piece of content generates, as well as where that traffic is coming from (search engines, social media, email, etc.). This helps you understand which content and promotional channels are most effective.

Engagement: Track engagement metrics like time spent on page, bounce rate, and social shares to gauge how well your audience is interacting with your content. High engagement indicates that your content is resonating with your audience.

Leads generated: Measure how many leads your content is generating. Track the number of email sign-ups, contact form submissions, or downloads that come from specific pieces of content.

Conversion rate: Your ultimate goal is to drive sales, so track how many people take the desired action after engaging with your content, whether it's making a purchase, booking a consultation, or signing up for a service.

ROI: Calculate the return on investment (ROI) of your content marketing efforts. This involves comparing the cost of creating and promoting content to the revenue generated from it. Understanding your ROI helps you determine which types of content are most cost-effective for driving sales.

By analyzing these metrics, you can identify which content is performing well and optimize your strategy to maximize results.

Content marketing is a powerful tool for solopreneurs to drive sales, build brand authority, and create meaningful connections with their audience. By understanding your audience, creating valuable content aligned with the buyer's journey, optimizing for SEO, and promoting your content strategically, you can attract potential customers and guide them toward making a purchase.

Remember, content marketing is a long-term strategy that requires consistency and patience. By consistently delivering high-quality content, nurturing leads, and tracking your results, you'll build a strong foundation for driving sales and growing your solopreneur business.

Email Marketing Strategies for Solopreneurs

Email marketing is one of the most powerful and cost-effective tools for solopreneurs to nurture relationships with their audience, promote products or services, and drive sales. With the ability to communicate directly with potential customers in their inbox, email marketing provides a personal touch and can generate high returns on investment (ROI). However, to be successful, it requires a well-thought-out strategy that aligns with your business goals and your audience's needs.

Here are email marketing strategies that solopreneurs can use to build and grow their business:

Build a High-Quality Email List

The success of your email marketing strategy starts with building a high-quality email list of people who are genuinely interested in your business. A large list of unengaged contacts is far less valuable than a smaller, engaged list of subscribers who are more likely to convert.

Here's how to grow your email list effectively:

Offer lead magnets: Lead magnets are free resources that you offer in exchange for a visitor's email address. Examples of lead magnets include eBooks, checklists, templates, webinars, or discounts. The key is to create a lead magnet that addresses a pain point or provides value to your target audience. For instance, a fitness coach might offer a free "7-Day Meal Plan" as a lead magnet.

Use sign-up forms on your website: Make it easy for website visitors to join your email list by placing sign-up forms in prominent locations on your site, such as the homepage, blog, or landing pages. Use compelling copy and a clear call-to-action (CTA) to encourage sign-ups, like "Get Your Free Guide" or "Join Our Community."

Pop-ups and exit-intent forms: Well-timed pop-ups can capture emails from visitors before they leave your website. Exit-intent pop-ups detect when a visitor is about to leave the page and offer a final opportunity to join your list by providing something of value.

Use social media: Promote your email list on your social media platforms. You can include a link to your email sign-up form in your bio, run giveaways, or create posts that highlight the benefits of joining your newsletter.

Leverage events and networking: If you host webinars, workshops, or attend networking events, use those opportunities to collect email addresses from potential clients or collaborators.

Building a high-quality list of engaged subscribers is key to a successful email marketing strategy because it ensures that the people receiving your emails are genuinely interested in your content and offerings.

SEGMENT YOUR AUDIENCE for Personalization

Not all of your subscribers have the same needs or interests, which is why segmenting your email list is essential. Segmentation allows you to send more personalized, relevant content to different groups of subscribers, increasing engagement and conversion rates.

Here are a few ways to segment your email list:

Demographics: Segment based on factors like age, location, or gender if relevant to your business. For example, if you sell products for both men and women, you could create separate email campaigns for each demographic.

Behavioral data: Segment your list based on how subscribers interact with your emails or website. For example, you can create a segment for people who have downloaded a lead magnet, made a purchase, or clicked on a specific link in an email.

Stage in the buyer's journey: Some subscribers may be new to your brand, while others may be loyal customers. Segmenting based on where they are in the buyer's journey allows you to send targeted messages that guide them through the sales funnel.

Interests and preferences: Ask your subscribers to indicate their interests or preferences when they sign up for your list. For instance, if you offer multiple services, you can allow subscribers to choose the specific topics they want to receive updates about.

By sending targeted and personalized emails, you can improve open and click-through rates, reduce unsubscribes, and increase the chances of converting leads into customers.

Craft Compelling and Relevant Content

The success of your email marketing campaign depends on the quality of the content you deliver. Your emails should be engaging, informative, and relevant to your audience's needs. Each email should provide value, whether that's through helpful tips, exclusive offers, or relevant news.

Here's how to create effective email content:

Write attention-grabbing subject lines: The subject line is the first thing subscribers see, and it plays a big role in whether or not they open your email. Craft subject lines that are clear, concise, and intriguing. You can also experiment with urgency, personalization, or curiosity to encourage opens. For example, "Last Chance: 20% Off Ends Today!" or "Get Your Free [Resource] Inside."

Deliver value upfront: Focus on providing value in every email. Whether it's a how-to guide, an exclusive discount, or industry insights, make sure that the content benefits the subscriber. This keeps your audience engaged and looking forward to future emails.

Use a conversational tone: Write your emails as if you're speaking to one person rather than a large group. A conversational, friendly tone helps build a personal connection with your audience. Solopreneurs often benefit from being relatable and approachable, so don't be afraid to inject personality into your emails.

Include clear CTAs: Each email should have a clear call-to-action (CTA) that tells subscribers what you want them to do next. Whether it's downloading a resource, signing up for a webinar, or purchasing a product, make the CTA easy to find and actionable. Use buttons, bold text, or colored links to make your CTAs stand out.

Incorporate visuals: Use visuals like images, videos, or infographics to make your emails more engaging and visually appealing. Just be mindful not to overload your emails with large files that could slow down loading times.

Use Automation to Nurture Leads

Email automation allows you to send timely, relevant emails to subscribers based on their actions or where they are in the sales funnel. Automation helps solopreneurs save time while maintaining consistent communication with their audience.

Here are a few ways to use email automation:

Welcome series: Create an automated welcome series for new subscribers. When someone joins your list, send a series of emails that introduce your brand, highlight your key offerings, and provide valuable resources. This helps nurture the relationship from the start and sets the tone for future communications.

Drip campaigns: A drip campaign is a series of pre-written emails that are sent out over a period of time. These emails can guide leads through the buyer's journey by delivering educational content, product information, testimonials, or offers. For example, if you're selling an online course, your drip campaign could include emails explaining the benefits, addressing common objections, and offering a discount.

Cart abandonment emails: If you have an e-commerce business, use automated cart abandonment emails to remind customers about the items they left in their shopping cart. These emails often include a friendly reminder and a CTA to complete the purchase. Offering an incentive like free shipping or a discount can also help encourage conversions.

Re-engagement emails: If certain subscribers haven't opened your emails in a while, set up an automated re-engagement campaign to win them back. Offer something special, like a limited-time discount or exclusive content, to re-engage them with your brand.

Automation helps you stay top-of-mind with your audience, nurture leads, and move potential customers closer to making a purchase.

Optimize for Mobile Devices

A large percentage of people check their emails on their smartphones, so it's essential to ensure that your emails are optimized for mobile devices. If your emails aren't mobile-friendly, you risk losing engagement or frustrating your subscribers.

Here's how to optimize your emails for mobile:

Use a responsive design: Ensure that your email template is responsive, meaning it automatically adjusts to fit the screen size of any device. Most email marketing platforms offer responsive templates, so choose one that looks good on both desktop and mobile.

Keep subject lines short: Since mobile screens display fewer characters than desktop, keep your subject lines short and to the point—ideally under 40 characters. This ensures that the entire subject line is visible on mobile devices.

Use large fonts and buttons: Make sure your text is large enough to be easily readable on a small screen. Use buttons instead of text links for your CTAs, and ensure that they are large enough to tap without difficulty.

Minimize images: While visuals are important, too many large images can slow down load times on mobile devices. Use images sparingly and make sure they are compressed for faster loading.

A/B Test Your Emails

A/B testing, also known as split testing, allows you to experiment with different elements of your emails to see what works best. By testing and analyzing the results, you can optimize your email campaigns for better engagement and conversion rates.

Here's how to conduct A/B testing:

Subject lines: Test different subject lines to see which ones get higher open rates. You can test length, tone, or the use of personalization.

Send times: Experiment with different days of the week and times of day to determine when your audience is most likely to engage with your emails.

CTAs: Test different call-to-action buttons or text to see which drives the most clicks. You can test the wording, color, size, or placement of your CTA.

Email content: You can also test the actual content of your email, such as the format, length, or inclusion of visuals. For example, test whether a short email with a direct CTA outperforms a longer, more detailed email.

By regularly testing and optimizing your emails, you can improve your email marketing performance and better understand what resonates with your audience.

Track and Analyze Your Results

To measure the effectiveness of your email marketing efforts, it's important to track key metrics and analyze the results. Most email marketing platforms provide analytics that give you insight into how your emails are performing.

Key metrics to track include:

Open rates: This metric tells you the percentage of people who opened your email. Low open rates can indicate that your subject lines or sender name aren't compelling enough, or that your email content isn't relevant to your audience.

Click-through rates (CTR): The click-through rate measures how many people clicked on a link or CTA within your email. A high CTR indicates that your content is engaging and your CTA is effective.

Conversion rates: This metric tracks how many people took the desired action after clicking on a link in your email, such as making a purchase or signing up for a service. This is one of the most important metrics to track, as it directly relates to sales.

Unsubscribe rates: While some unsubscribes are normal, a high unsubscribe rate could indicate that your content isn't relevant or you're sending emails too frequently. Pay attention to feedback and adjust your strategy if needed.

Bounce rates: This metric measures how many of your emails couldn't be delivered. High bounce rates can affect your email deliverability, so regularly clean your list to remove invalid or inactive email addresses.

By analyzing these metrics, you can refine your email marketing strategy, improve engagement, and ultimately drive more sales.

Email marketing is a powerful tool for solopreneurs to connect with their audience, build trust, and drive sales. By building a high-quality email list, personalizing your content through segmentation, and using automation to nurture leads, you can create an effective email marketing strategy that supports your business growth. Regular testing, optimizing for mobile, and analyzing your results will help you refine your approach and ensure that your emails are delivering real value to your subscribers. With the right strategy, email marketing can become one of the most valuable assets in your solopreneur toolkit.

Creating an Engaged Community around Your Brand

Creating an engaged community around your brand is essential for solopreneurs who want to build long-term relationships with their customers and foster brand loyalty. An engaged community not only amplifies your reach but also helps create a sense of belonging and trust, turning customers into advocates who promote your business organically. Building a community takes time and consistent effort, but the rewards are invaluable for your brand's growth.

Here's how you can create an engaged community around your solopreneur brand:

Define Your Brand's Purpose and Values

Before building a community, it's crucial to define what your brand stands for and why people should rally around it. Your brand's purpose and values will serve as the foundation of your community and help attract like-minded individuals who resonate with your mission.

Here's how to define your brand's purpose:

Identify your "why": What is the core reason your business exists? Beyond making a profit, think about the impact you want to make in your industry or in your customers' lives. For example, if you're a solopreneur in the fitness industry, your purpose might be to help people live healthier, more balanced lives.

Establish your values: Your brand values reflect what you believe in and guide how you operate your business. Are you committed to sustainability, creativity, or innovation? Define a set of core values that align with your brand's mission and communicate them consistently through your messaging and actions.

Share your story: People connect with stories more than they do with products or services. Share your personal story as a solopreneur—why you started your business, the challenges you've faced, and the impact you hope to have. This helps humanize your brand and creates a deeper connection with your audience.

Once your brand's purpose and values are clearly defined, you'll attract an audience that shares your beliefs, making it easier to build an engaged and loyal community.

Understand Your Audience's Needs and Interests

To create an engaged community, you need to understand who your audience is and what matters most to them. The more you know about your target audience, the better you can create content and experiences that resonate with them.

Here's how to better understand your audience:

Create audience personas: Develop detailed profiles of your ideal customers, including their demographics, interests, challenges, and goals. This helps you tailor your content and community-building efforts to their specific needs.

Engage directly with your audience: Use social media, surveys, and polls to ask your audience what they care about, what challenges they face, and what kind of content or support they're looking for. Regularly interact with your community by responding to comments and messages, and use their feedback to shape your content.

Analyze audience behavior: Pay attention to how your audience engages with your content, products, or services. What types of posts get the most likes, shares, or comments? What content generates the most questions or feedback? These insights will help you refine your approach and deliver more value to your community.

By deeply understanding your audience's needs, you can create a brand community that feels personalized and aligned with their interests, making them more likely to engage with and support your business.

Leverage Social Media to Foster Engagement

Social media is one of the most powerful tools for building and nurturing a brand community. It provides a platform for real-time interaction and enables you to create a space where your audience can connect with both your brand and each other.

Here's how to leverage social media to build an engaged community:

Choose the right platforms: Focus on the social media platforms where your target audience is most active. For example, Instagram is great for visual brands, while LinkedIn is ideal for B2B businesses. Don't spread yourself too thin—concentrate on one or two platforms where you can be consistent and active.

Create a content plan: Develop a content strategy that encourages interaction and provides value. Share a mix of content types, including educational posts, behind-the-scenes content, customer stories, and questions that spark conversation. Use engaging formats like polls, Q&A sessions, and live videos to keep your audience involved.

Use hashtags and challenges: Create a branded hashtag that encourages your community to share their experiences with your products or services. You can also launch social media challenges that invite your audience to participate and contribute, which can boost engagement and visibility. For example, if you run a fitness brand, you could create a "30-Day Fitness Challenge" that encourages followers to post their progress using a specific hashtag.

Foster a two-way conversation: Social media isn't just about posting content—it's about creating dialogue. Respond to comments, ask questions, and encourage your audience to share their opinions. The more your community feels heard and valued, the more engaged they will be.

By consistently showing up on social media and fostering genuine conversations, you can turn followers into active participants who feel connected to your brand and its values.

Create a Private Community Space

While social media is a great tool for building a broad audience, creating a private space—like a Facebook Group, Discord server, or community forum—allows you to foster deeper connections and cultivate a sense of exclusivity within your brand community.

Here's how to create and nurture a private community:

Choose the right platform: Depending on your business, you can create a Facebook Group, a LinkedIn Group, or use platforms like Slack or Discord for more interactive discussions. Choose a platform that aligns with the way your audience prefers to communicate.

Set clear community guidelines: To create a positive, engaging environment, set guidelines that outline the purpose of the group and the behavior expected from members. For example, you might encourage collaboration, sharing, and mutual support, while discouraging negativity or self-promotion.

Provide exclusive content and perks: Offer your community members something valuable in exchange for joining the group, such as exclusive content, early access to products, or special discounts. This creates a sense of belonging and makes your community feel like a VIP experience.

Host regular events and discussions: Keep your community engaged by hosting regular events, such as live Q&A sessions, webinars, workshops, or member spotlights. Encourage members to participate in discussions, share their experiences, and ask questions.

By creating a private space for your community, you build a stronger sense of belonging and connection, which increases engagement and loyalty.

Encourage User-Generated Content (UGC)

User-generated content (UGC) is content created by your audience that showcases their experience with your brand. UGC not only helps build trust and authenticity but also turns your customers into advocates who spread the word about your business.

Here's how to encourage user-generated content:

Create a branded hashtag: Encourage your community to use a specific hashtag when they share posts related to your brand. This makes it easy for you to find and share their content while giving them recognition.

Feature customer stories: Highlight your customers by sharing their stories or testimonials on your website, social media, or email newsletters. Featuring UGC not only rewards loyal customers but also shows potential customers how others benefit from your products or services.

Run contests or giveaways: Host contests that encourage your audience to create content around a specific theme related to your brand. For example, you could ask them to share how they use your product in their daily lives or post before-and-after photos showing their results. Offer prizes to incentivize participation.

Celebrate community milestones: Recognize your community's contributions by celebrating milestones such as reaching a certain number of posts, members, or followers. Acknowledge the role your audience plays in your brand's growth and show your appreciation for their support.

User-generated content helps amplify your message and builds a stronger connection with your audience, as it shows that real people trust and support your brand.

Be Authentic and Consistent

Authenticity is at the heart of building an engaged community. People want to connect with brands that are genuine and transparent, not just businesses trying to make a sale. As a solopreneur, your authenticity is one of your greatest assets, so let your personality and values shine through in everything you do.

Here's how to build trust and authenticity with your community:

Be transparent: Share your journey as a solopreneur—the successes, challenges, and lessons learned. Transparency fosters trust, and your audience will appreciate your honesty and willingness to show the human side of your brand.

Stay consistent: Building a community takes time and effort, so consistency is key. Show up regularly, whether it's through social media posts, newsletters, or community discussions. Consistency helps build momentum and keeps your community engaged over the long term.

Respond to feedback: Be open to feedback from your community, both positive and negative. Listen to their suggestions, address concerns, and make changes when necessary. Showing that you value their input strengthens the bond between your brand and your audience.

Celebrate your community: Regularly acknowledge and celebrate your community members. Whether it's through shout-outs, special offers, or simply thanking them for their support, showing appreciation fosters loyalty and engagement.

When you're authentic and consistent, your community will feel more connected to you and your brand, leading to deeper engagement and long-term loyalty.

Provide Value Consistently

At the core of any engaged community is the value that you provide. If you consistently deliver value—whether through educational content, helpful resources, or entertainment—your audience will keep coming back and remain engaged with your brand.

Here's how to consistently provide value to your community:

Offer exclusive content: Create valuable content that is only available to your community members. This could include webinars, downloadable resources, or behind-the-scenes looks at your business.

Host events: Organize virtual events like Q&A sessions, workshops, or webinars that offer your community the opportunity to learn and interact with you directly. These events provide value while also deepening the connection between your brand and your audience.

Provide practical tips and advice: Share actionable insights that help your audience solve problems, improve their lives, or reach their goals. For example, if you're a business coach, you might offer tips on productivity or business growth.

Create a resource library: Develop a collection of valuable resources, such as templates, guides, or checklists, that your community members can access at any time. Providing useful tools fosters goodwill and positions you as an authority in your niche.

By consistently delivering value, you'll keep your community engaged and position your brand as a valuable resource in their lives.

Creating an engaged community around your brand is one of the most powerful ways to build loyalty, generate word-of-mouth marketing, and foster meaningful relationships with your audience. By defining your brand's purpose, understanding your audience's needs, leveraging social media, and encouraging user-generated content, you can cultivate a community that is not only engaged but also deeply invested in your brand's success. As a solopreneur, your authenticity and personal touch are invaluable assets that can help you stand out and connect with your audience on a deeper level. Through consistency, transparency, and a commitment to providing value, you can build a community that supports your business and helps you grow in ways that go beyond just sales.

Exploring Distribution Techniques and Channels

For solopreneurs, finding the right distribution techniques and channels is essential to getting products and services into the hands of your target audience. Whether you're selling physical goods, digital products, or services, understanding how to effectively distribute your offerings can make a significant difference in your business's success. With the rise of digital platforms and the evolution of traditional channels, solopreneurs now have more options than ever to reach customers globally.

Here's how you can explore and leverage distribution techniques and channels to maximize your reach and drive sales.

Understand Your Distribution Options

Before diving into specific channels, it's important to understand the two main types of distribution: **direct** and **indirect**. Each comes with its own advantages and considerations for solopreneurs.

Direct distribution: In direct distribution, you sell your products or services directly to your customers without intermediaries. This method allows you to maintain control over pricing, customer experience, and branding. Direct distribution can take place through your own website, e-commerce platform, social media, or physical location.

Indirect distribution: Indirect distribution involves third-party intermediaries, such as wholesalers, retailers, or marketplaces, to distribute your products. While this method can help you reach a broader audience, it often involves giving up some control over pricing and customer relationships, and you may also need to share profits with the intermediaries.

Understanding which approach suits your business will depend on your target audience, product type, and resources. Many solopreneurs use a combination of both direct and indirect distribution to maximize reach.

Use Your Own Website for Direct Sales

One of the most effective direct distribution channels for solopreneurs is your own website. Having a dedicated website allows you to control the customer journey, from browsing your products or services to completing a purchase. It also helps you build your brand and establish trust with your audience.

Here's how to make the most of your website for direct sales:

E-commerce integration: If you sell physical or digital products, use e-commerce platforms like Shopify, WooCommerce (for WordPress), or BigCommerce to turn your website into a full-fledged online store. These platforms offer tools for managing inventory, processing payments, and tracking orders, making it easier to handle sales on your own.

Service-based sales: For solopreneurs offering services like consulting, coaching, or freelancing, integrate booking tools or forms that allow potential clients to schedule appointments, book consultations, or request quotes directly through your website.

Content marketing: Your website can also serve as a hub for content marketing, such as blog posts, videos, or case studies. By creating valuable content that draws in visitors, you can nurture leads and direct them to your products or services. This is especially effective for solopreneurs offering knowledge-based services.

Email capture: Use email marketing strategies to capture leads on your website, such as offering a lead magnet in exchange for their email address. You can then nurture those leads through email campaigns, promoting your products and services directly to them.

Leverage Online Marketplaces

Online marketplaces are a popular indirect distribution channel that allows solopreneurs to reach a wide audience without the need to manage their own e-commerce infrastructure. These platforms can provide valuable exposure and streamline sales processes, but they come with fees and competition.

Here are some popular online marketplaces to consider:

Amazon: As one of the largest e-commerce platforms in the world, Amazon provides access to millions of customers. It's particularly useful for solopreneurs selling physical products. You can choose between selling directly through Amazon's marketplace or using their fulfillment service (FBA) to handle shipping and logistics.

Etsy: Ideal for solopreneurs selling handmade, vintage, or craft items, Etsy is a global marketplace that caters to creative entrepreneurs. It's a great option if your products align with Etsy's niche audience, and the platform makes it easy to set up and manage a shop.

eBay: Another popular marketplace, eBay allows you to sell new or used products through auctions or fixed-price listings. It's a good option for solopreneurs with unique, one-of-a-kind items or those looking to sell to a global audience.

Gumroad: For solopreneurs selling digital products like eBooks, courses, or software, Gumroad offers a simple platform to manage digital sales. It's especially useful for creators and artists who want to sell their work without setting up a full e-commerce site.

Udemy and Teachable: If you're selling online courses, platforms like Udemy and Teachable provide the infrastructure to create, host, and sell your courses to a global audience. These platforms handle payment processing, course delivery, and marketing, making it easy for solopreneurs to focus on creating content.

While online marketplaces offer access to a broad audience, keep in mind that they often charge fees or commissions on each sale, so factor these costs into your pricing strategy.

Sell Through Social Media Platforms

Social media platforms have evolved into powerful distribution channels for solopreneurs, allowing you to sell directly to your audience while building brand awareness. Whether you're selling physical products, digital goods, or services, platforms like Instagram, Facebook, and Pinterest offer tools to help you reach and convert customers.

Here's how to sell through social media:

Instagram Shopping: Instagram allows you to create shoppable posts that let users purchase products directly from your feed. You can tag products in your posts, Stories, and even in videos, making it easy for followers to explore and buy from your store.

Facebook Shops: With Facebook Shops, you can create an online storefront that integrates with your Facebook and Instagram profiles. It's a great way to showcase your products and services, engage with customers, and drive sales through social media.

Pinterest Buyable Pins: Pinterest's audience is highly motivated to purchase, making it an ideal platform for solopreneurs selling physical products. With Buyable Pins, you can allow users to purchase directly from Pinterest without leaving the platform.

TikTok and YouTube: For solopreneurs offering products or services that lend themselves to visual storytelling, platforms like TikTok and YouTube can be valuable distribution channels. You can create engaging video content that showcases your offerings and drive traffic to your website or marketplace listings.

To maximize sales through social media, be consistent with posting and interacting with your followers, use relevant hashtags to increase discoverability, and leverage paid social media advertising to target your ideal audience.

Explore Affiliate Marketing and Partnerships

Affiliate marketing is a powerful distribution technique where other people (affiliates) promote your products or services in exchange for a commission on each sale they generate. It's a low-risk way to expand your reach and grow your sales without upfront advertising costs.

Here's how to set up an affiliate marketing program:

Choose an affiliate platform: Platforms like ShareASale, CJ Affiliate, and Rakuten make it easy to set up and manage your affiliate program. These platforms allow you to track sales, manage affiliates, and process commissions.

Offer competitive commissions: To attract affiliates, offer a competitive commission rate based on the value of your product or service. For digital products, commission rates can be as high as 30–50%, while for physical products, they are typically lower.

Partner with influencers: Influencer marketing is a form of affiliate marketing where social media influencers promote your products or services to their audience. Look for influencers whose audience aligns with your target market and offer them an affiliate partnership.

Leverage your existing network: You can also reach out to industry peers, bloggers, and content creators within your niche to become affiliates. They can promote your products through blog posts, email campaigns, or social media, helping you tap into new audiences.

Affiliate marketing is especially effective for solopreneurs offering digital products or courses, as affiliates can promote your offerings to large audiences with little ongoing effort from you.

Utilize Email Marketing for Direct Distribution

Email marketing remains one of the most effective ways to directly distribute your products or services. As a solopreneur, building and nurturing an email list allows you to maintain a personal connection with your audience and promote your offerings directly to them.

Here's how to use email marketing for distribution:

Create targeted email campaigns: Segment your email list based on factors like past purchases, interests, or engagement levels, and send personalized offers that appeal to each group. For example, if you're launching a new product, you can send early access offers or discounts to your most loyal customers.

Automate email sequences: Use email automation tools to set up sequences that nurture leads, follow up with potential customers, or promote new products. Automated emails, such as welcome sequences, cart abandonment emails, or product launch sequences, can help drive sales without manual effort.

Promote limited-time offers: Time-sensitive promotions, such as flash sales or holiday discounts, can create a sense of urgency and drive immediate sales. Use your email list to announce these offers and encourage your subscribers to take action.

Provide exclusive content: Reward your email subscribers with exclusive content, such as behind-the-scenes looks, product previews, or discounts. This not only helps build a loyal customer base but also drives more direct sales from your email campaigns.

Consider Local and Pop-Up Distribution

If you sell physical products, don't overlook the value of local distribution channels. Selling your products in-person through pop-up shops, local markets, or retail partnerships can help you reach new customers and build a stronger connection with your community.

HERE ARE SOME LOCAL distribution ideas:

Pop-up shops: Partner with local businesses or venues to set up temporary retail spaces where you can showcase your products. Pop-up shops create a sense of urgency and exclusivity, which can drive sales and attract new customers.

Local markets: Many solopreneurs find success selling at farmers markets, craft fairs, or local events. These venues allow you to interact with customers face-to-face, build brand awareness, and gather direct feedback.

Retail partnerships: Consider partnering with local boutiques or retailers to stock your products. Many independent stores are open to collaborating with local brands, allowing you to reach new audiences without having to manage your own storefront.

Workshops or events: Hosting workshops or events related to your product or service can also serve as a distribution channel. For example, if you sell wellness products, you could host a health workshop where attendees can purchase your products on-site.

While these local distribution channels may require more effort than online sales, they can help you build deeper relationships with your customers and create memorable experiences around your brand.

Explore International Distribution

If your products or services have global appeal, international distribution channels can help you reach new markets. Expanding beyond your home country can increase your customer base and create new revenue streams.

Here's how to explore international distribution:

Use global e-commerce platforms: Platforms like Amazon, Etsy, and eBay have global marketplaces, allowing you to sell to customers worldwide. These platforms handle international payments and shipping logistics, making it easier for solopreneurs to expand internationally.

Work with international distributors: If you sell physical products, consider partnering with international distributors who can help get your products into foreign markets. These distributors have local knowledge and established networks, making it easier for your brand to enter new regions.

Ensure compliance with international regulations: Selling internationally requires you to comply with different countries' tax laws, shipping regulations, and customs requirements. Make sure you understand the legal and logistical aspects of international sales before expanding.

Exploring and utilizing the right distribution techniques and channels is key to scaling your solopreneur business and reaching a broader audience. Whether you choose to sell directly through your website, leverage online marketplaces, or build relationships through social media and local events, it's important to find the mix that works best for your business model and target audience.

How to Set Up and Run an E-Commerce Store

Setting up and running an e-commerce store is an essential step for solopreneurs who want to sell products or services online. An e-commerce store allows you to reach a global audience, manage sales efficiently, and provide a seamless shopping experience for your customers. Whether you're selling physical goods, digital products, or services, creating an online store can be a game-changer for your business.

Here's a comprehensive guide on how to set up and run a successful e-commerce store:

Choose the Right E-Commerce Platform

The first step in setting up your e-commerce store is selecting the right platform. There are several e-commerce platforms available, each with its own features and benefits. When choosing a platform, consider factors such as ease of use, scalability, customization options, and pricing.

Here are some popular e-commerce platforms for solopreneurs:

Shopify: One of the most popular e-commerce platforms, Shopify is known for its ease of use and robust features. It offers everything you need to set up an online store, including payment processing, inventory management, and customizable templates. Shopify is a great option for beginners and solopreneurs who want a user-friendly platform.

WooCommerce: If you already have a WordPress website, WooCommerce is a powerful plugin that can turn your site into an online store. It offers full customization and integrates seamlessly with WordPress, making it ideal for solopreneurs who want more control over their store's design and functionality.

BigCommerce: BigCommerce is another comprehensive platform that's suitable for solopreneurs who need a scalable solution. It offers built-in SEO features, customizable themes, and multi-channel selling capabilities, allowing you to sell across platforms like Amazon, eBay, and Facebook.

Squarespace: Known for its beautifully designed templates, Squarespace is a good option for creative entrepreneurs who prioritize aesthetics. It's easy to set up and offers integrated e-commerce features, making it a solid choice for solopreneurs who want a visually appealing store.

Etsy: If you're selling handmade or vintage products, Etsy provides an easy way to start selling online. While it's a marketplace rather than a traditional e-commerce platform, it's ideal for solopreneurs in creative industries who want to tap into a niche audience.

Choose a platform that best fits your business model, products, and technical expertise. Each platform offers different levels of customization, so consider how much control you want over your store's design and functionality.

SELECT YOUR PRODUCTS and Plan Your Inventory

Before launching your e-commerce store, you need to decide what products you'll sell and how you'll manage inventory. Whether you're offering physical products, digital goods, or services, careful planning is essential for a smooth operation.

Here's how to plan your product offerings and inventory:

Decide what to sell: Choose products that align with your brand, expertise, and audience's needs. If you're a solopreneur with a passion for crafting, you might sell handmade goods, while a digital marketer might sell online courses or eBooks. Be clear about the value your products offer to your target customers.

Source products: If you're selling physical goods, decide how you'll source your products. Will you make them yourself, work with manufacturers, or use a dropshipping model? Dropshipping allows you to sell products without holding inventory, as your supplier handles fulfillment on your behalf.

Set up inventory management: Managing inventory is critical for ensuring you don't oversell or run out of stock. Most e-commerce platforms offer built-in inventory management tools that help you track stock levels, set reorder points, and notify you when products are running low. If you're using dropshipping, your supplier will handle inventory management.

Create product descriptions: Write clear, compelling product descriptions that highlight the features and benefits of each item. Focus on how your products solve a problem or fulfill a need for your customers. Include relevant keywords to improve search engine optimization (SEO) and help customers find your products more easily.

Use high-quality images: Product images are essential for an e-commerce store, as they provide customers with a visual representation of what they're buying. Invest in high-quality images that showcase your products from different angles and in use. If possible, include videos or customer reviews with images to boost trust.

Design Your E-Commerce Store

Your store's design plays a major role in attracting customers and providing a seamless shopping experience. A well-designed store makes it easy for visitors to browse products, find information, and make purchases.

Here's how to design an effective e-commerce store:

Choose a template: Most e-commerce platforms offer customizable templates that allow you to create a professional-looking store without any coding skills. Choose a template that reflects your brand's style and is easy to navigate. Make sure it's mobile-friendly, as many customers will shop from their phones.

Create a user-friendly layout: Design your store with the customer experience in mind. Make sure your navigation is clear and easy to use, with categories and filters that help visitors find what they're looking for quickly. Your home page should highlight key products or promotions, and your product pages should be easy to read with clear calls to action.

Focus on branding: Consistent branding helps build trust and familiarity with your audience. Use your brand's colors, fonts, and logo throughout your site to create a cohesive experience. Your branding should reflect your values and appeal to your target audience.

Optimize for conversions: Make it easy for customers to complete their purchase by optimizing your checkout process. Minimize the number of steps required to complete a purchase, and offer guest checkout for those who don't want to create an account. Provide multiple payment options, such as credit cards, PayPal, and Apple Pay, to accommodate different preferences.

Set Up Payment Gateways and Shipping

Once your store is designed, it's time to set up the infrastructure that allows customers to pay for products and receive their orders. A seamless payment and shipping process is crucial for building customer trust and ensuring repeat business.

Here's how to set up payments and shipping:

Choose payment gateways: A payment gateway processes credit card transactions and transfers funds to your account. Popular payment gateways include PayPal, Stripe, and Square, all of which integrate with most e-commerce platforms. Choose a payment gateway that is secure, easy to use, and supports multiple currencies if you plan to sell internationally.

Calculate shipping rates: If you're selling physical products, you'll need to calculate how much it costs to ship orders to your customers. Most e-commerce platforms allow you to set up flat-rate, real-time, or free shipping options. You can integrate with carriers like USPS, UPS, or FedEx to automatically calculate shipping rates based on location and package weight.

Offer shipping options: Provide customers with a range of shipping options, such as standard, express, or free shipping for orders over a certain amount. Offering free or discounted shipping can be a powerful incentive for customers to complete their purchases.

Handle international shipping: If you're selling to international customers, make sure you understand the shipping costs, customs duties, and delivery times for different regions. Many e-commerce platforms allow you to set different shipping rates for domestic and international orders.

Manage taxes: Depending on where your business is located and where you're selling, you may need to charge sales tax or VAT (value-added tax). Most e-commerce platforms can automatically calculate taxes based on the customer's location, so make sure to configure your tax settings correctly.

Implement SEO and Content Marketing

Driving traffic to your e-commerce store requires a strong marketing strategy. Search engine optimization (SEO) and content marketing are two of the most effective ways to attract organic traffic and boost sales.

Here's how to implement SEO and content marketing:

Optimize product pages for SEO: Use relevant keywords in your product titles, descriptions, and meta tags to improve your search engine rankings. Each product page should have a unique title and description that includes the primary keywords customers are likely to search for.

Create a blog: Content marketing is a powerful way to drive traffic to your store and engage with your audience. Start a blog on your website and create articles related to your products or industry. For example, if you sell fitness equipment, you could write blog posts about workout routines or fitness tips. Blog posts not only help with SEO but also position you as an expert in your niche.

Use internal and external links: Include internal links within your site to direct visitors to relevant products or blog posts. External links to authoritative sources can also improve your site's SEO. For example, link to product reviews, industry news, or helpful guides that provide value to your customers.

Utilize social media: Share your blog posts, products, and promotions on social media platforms like Instagram, Facebook, and Pinterest to drive traffic to your store. Consistently engage with your audience by posting valuable content and responding to comments or questions.

Launch Your E-Commerce Store

Once your e-commerce store is set up and optimized, it's time to launch. However, before going live, ensure that everything is working smoothly by conducting thorough testing.

Here's how to successfully launch your store:

Test the checkout process: Make sure your payment gateways are working, and test the entire checkout process to ensure it's smooth and free of issues. Try purchasing a product as if you were a customer to catch any potential errors.

Check for mobile responsiveness: Ensure that your e-commerce site looks and functions well on all devices, including smartphones and tablets. Since many customers shop from their mobile devices, this step is crucial for a successful launch.

Promote your launch: Use email marketing and social media to announce your store's launch to your audience. Offer special promotions or discounts to incentivize first-time customers. You can also create countdowns, teasers, or sneak peeks to build excitement before your launch date.

Set up analytics: Use tools like Google Analytics or the analytics features provided by your e-commerce platform to track visitor behavior, sales, and conversions. Monitoring your data helps you understand how customers are interacting with your site and where improvements can be made.

Provide Excellent Customer Service

Great customer service is key to running a successful e-commerce store. Providing a seamless shopping experience and addressing customer concerns promptly can lead to repeat business and positive word-of-mouth referrals.

Here's how to provide excellent customer service:

Offer multiple contact options: Make it easy for customers to reach you with questions or concerns. Provide contact options such as email, phone, or live chat, and respond promptly to inquiries.

Create a comprehensive FAQ page: Anticipate common questions and provide answers on your website's FAQ page. This can help customers find the information they need without having to contact you directly.

Set clear return and refund policies: Be transparent about your return and refund policies. Provide clear instructions for returning products, and offer hassle-free returns to build trust with your customers.

Follow up after purchases: Send automated follow-up emails to customers after they make a purchase, thanking them for their order and offering additional support if needed. You can also encourage customers to leave reviews or share their experiences on social media.

Scale and Grow Your E-Commerce Business

Once your store is up and running, the focus shifts to scaling and growing your business. This involves continuously refining your marketing efforts, expanding your product offerings, and optimizing the customer experience.

Here are strategies to grow your e-commerce business:

Expand your product line: Once you've established a customer base, consider adding complementary products or services to your store. Expanding your product line can attract repeat customers and increase your average order value.

Use paid advertising: Invest in paid advertising, such as Google Ads, Facebook Ads, or Instagram Ads, to reach a larger audience and drive traffic to your store. Paid ads can help you target specific demographics and increase conversions.

Leverage email marketing: Build an email list and use it to send targeted campaigns, promote new products, or offer exclusive discounts. Email marketing is one of the most effective ways to nurture leads and turn them into repeat customers.

Offer loyalty programs: Create a loyalty program that rewards customers for making repeat purchases. Offer points, discounts, or free products as incentives to encourage customer retention.

Analyze and optimize: Regularly review your analytics to identify areas for improvement. Track conversion rates, cart abandonment, and customer behavior to make data-driven decisions that enhance your store's performance.

Setting up and running an e-commerce store can be a highly rewarding venture for solopreneurs. By choosing the right platform, planning your inventory, optimizing your store's design, and implementing effective marketing strategies, you can create a seamless shopping experience that drives sales and builds a loyal customer base. As you grow, focus on providing excellent customer service and continuously refining your operations to scale your business successfully.

Separating Business from Home Life: Work-Life Balance Tips

For solopreneurs, separating business from home life can be particularly challenging, as the boundaries between personal and professional spaces often blur when you're running a business from home. Achieving a healthy work-life balance is essential for maintaining productivity, reducing stress, and fostering personal well-being. While it's tempting to constantly focus on your business, finding time for yourself, your family, and personal interests is just as important for long-term success.

Here are practical tips to help solopreneurs separate business from home life and maintain a healthy work-life balance:

Establish a Dedicated Workspace

One of the most effective ways to separate business from home life is to create a designated workspace that's solely used for work. This not only helps you mentally switch between work mode and personal time but also improves productivity by creating a structured environment.

Here's how to create a dedicated workspace:

Choose a specific room or area: Ideally, set up your workspace in a separate room with a door to create physical boundaries between work and home life. If you don't have a spare room, designate a specific corner or area of your home as your office space.

Keep work materials in the workspace: Store all your work-related materials, such as your laptop, notebooks, and documents, in your designated workspace. Avoid letting work items spill over into your living room or bedroom, which can blur the boundaries between work and relaxation.

Make it comfortable and functional: Invest in an ergonomic chair, a sturdy desk, and proper lighting to ensure you're comfortable while working. A well-organized, comfortable workspace makes it easier to focus during work hours and leave work behind when you're done.

Set office hours: Even though you're working from home, establish regular office hours just as you would if you were working in a traditional office. This helps create a routine and signals to both you and your family when it's time to work and when it's time to unwind.

Create a Structured Routine

Having a structured daily routine is essential for maintaining a balance between business and home life. Without a clear schedule, it's easy for work to bleed into your personal time or for distractions at home to interfere with your productivity.

Here's how to create a structured routine:

Set consistent working hours: Establish regular working hours and stick to them as much as possible. This creates a clear boundary between work time and personal time, allowing you to focus fully on each without feeling overwhelmed.

Start your day with a morning routine: A morning routine helps you transition into work mode. Whether it's exercising, meditating, or having a cup of coffee, starting your day with a consistent ritual can improve focus and set a productive tone for the day.

Plan breaks throughout the day: Schedule short breaks throughout your workday to rest and recharge. A break could be as simple as stepping away from your desk for a few minutes, stretching, or going for a short walk. Taking regular breaks prevents burnout and keeps you mentally fresh.

End your workday with a closing routine: Just as you start your day with a routine, create a ritual to signal the end of your workday. This could be closing your laptop, organizing your workspace, or writing a to-do list for the next day. A clear closing routine helps you mentally shift from work mode to relaxation.

Set Boundaries with Family and Friends

Working from home can sometimes lead to interruptions and distractions from family members, roommates, or friends who may not understand your need for focus. Setting clear boundaries with those around you is crucial for maintaining productivity and work-life balance.

Here's how to set boundaries with family and friends:

Communicate your work hours: Let your family and friends know your working hours and explain that during this time, you need to focus on your business. Establishing these expectations early on helps prevent interruptions during work hours.

Create visual cues: Use visual cues to signal when you're working. For example, closing the door to your workspace or wearing noise-cancelling headphones can be a clear sign to others that you're not available for non-work-related conversations.

Schedule personal time: Set aside specific times in your schedule for family and social activities. By creating designated times for personal life, you'll be able to fully engage with your loved ones without worrying about work.

Address boundaries with children: If you have children at home, it's important to explain the concept of work hours in a way they can understand. Set rules around when they can interrupt and when they should wait until you're on a break. You can also set up activities to keep them engaged while you're working.

Learn to Say No

As a solopreneur, you may feel pressure to say "yes" to every opportunity or client request, fearing that turning down work could hurt your business. However, overcommitting can quickly lead to burnout and negatively impact both your professional and personal life.

Here's how to say no while maintaining balance:

Prioritize your tasks: Review your commitments and focus on the tasks that are most important for growing your business. Don't be afraid to say no to non-essential projects or requests that don't align with your goals or capacity.

Set realistic expectations: When taking on new clients or projects, be upfront about your availability and timeline. Setting realistic expectations from the start helps prevent last-minute demands that could interfere with your work-life balance.

Delegate when possible: If you're feeling overwhelmed, consider outsourcing or delegating certain tasks. Hiring a virtual assistant or freelancer to handle administrative work or specialized tasks can free up more time for you to focus on what truly matters.

Avoid over-scheduling: Be mindful of your time and avoid overloading your schedule with back-to-back commitments. Leave buffer time between meetings or tasks so you have room to breathe and adjust to unexpected events.

Use Technology to Your Advantage

Technology can be both a blessing and a curse for solopreneurs. On one hand, it allows you to run your business from anywhere, but on the other hand, it can make it difficult to disconnect from work. The key is to use technology strategically to boost productivity while ensuring you have time to unplug.

Here's how to use technology effectively:

Automate repetitive tasks: Use automation tools to streamline repetitive tasks such as invoicing, scheduling, or social media management. Automating these tasks frees up more time for you to focus on high-value activities or personal time.

Set email boundaries: Avoid checking emails outside of your designated work hours. You can set up auto-responders to let clients know when they can expect a response or use a separate email account for personal communication to avoid work-related distractions during personal time.

Use time management apps: Time management apps like Trello, Asana, or Todoist can help you stay organized and on track with your tasks. Use these tools to break down your day into manageable tasks and set reminders for important deadlines.

Limit screen time after work: Set limits on your screen time once you've finished work for the day. Constantly checking your phone or laptop for work notifications can prevent you from fully relaxing and enjoying personal time. Consider turning off notifications or setting your phone to "Do Not Disturb" mode during non-work hours.

Schedule Time for Self-Care

Maintaining a healthy work-life balance requires making self-care a priority. Taking time to recharge, relax, and engage in activities that nourish your mind and body helps prevent burnout and ensures you're at your best both professionally and personally.

Here's how to prioritize self-care as a solopreneur:

Exercise regularly: Incorporate physical activity into your daily routine, whether it's going for a walk, practicing yoga, or hitting the gym. Exercise helps reduce stress, boost energy levels, and improve mental clarity, all of which are important for solopreneurs juggling multiple responsibilities.

Practice mindfulness or meditation: Mindfulness practices such as meditation, deep breathing, or journaling can help you stay grounded and manage stress. Taking even a few minutes each day to quiet your mind can improve your focus and emotional well-being.

Schedule leisure time: Block out time in your schedule for hobbies, relaxation, or socializing with friends and family. Engaging in non-work activities that bring you joy is important for maintaining balance and avoiding burnout.

Take regular vacations: Don't hesitate to take time off, even if it's just for a short weekend getaway or a day off. Taking a break from work allows you to return feeling refreshed and more motivated. Plan vacations or personal time in advance to ensure you don't neglect your need for rest.

Set Clear Work-Life Boundaries

Setting boundaries around when and where you work is essential for maintaining a work-life balance. Without clear boundaries, it's easy for your business to spill over into every aspect of your life, leaving you feeling constantly "on" and unable to disconnect.

Here's how to set clear work-life boundaries:

Avoid working outside of your set hours: Resist the temptation to work late into the night or during weekends. Once your work hours are over, close your laptop, put away your work materials, and focus on personal time. Establishing clear boundaries helps prevent burnout and promotes a healthier work-life balance.

Set boundaries with clients: Be upfront with clients about your availability and work hours. Let them know when they can expect responses to emails or calls, and make it clear that you won't be available outside of those hours unless it's an emergency.

Create a separation ritual: Having a separation ritual at the end of your workday helps create a clear transition from work to personal time. This could be something simple like tidying up your workspace, going for a walk, or spending time with family. A separation ritual signals to your brain that the workday is over and it's time to unwind.

Regularly Evaluate Your Work-Life Balance

Maintaining a healthy work-life balance is an ongoing process that requires regular evaluation and adjustment. Life circumstances, business demands, and personal needs change over time, so it's important to periodically assess how well you're balancing your work and personal life.

Here's how to evaluate and adjust your work-life balance:

Reflect on your priorities: Take time to regularly reflect on your personal and professional priorities. Are you spending enough time with family or pursuing personal interests? If you find that work is taking up too much of your time, it may be necessary to reallocate your schedule or adjust your workload.

Assess your stress levels: Monitor your stress levels and overall well-being. If you're feeling overwhelmed, burnt out, or constantly tired, it may be a sign that your work-life balance needs adjustment. Pay attention to how your work habits impact your physical and mental health.

Make changes when needed: Don't be afraid to make changes to your routine, workload, or boundaries if you're struggling to maintain balance. Whether it's outsourcing certain tasks, taking a break, or adjusting your work hours, making small changes can significantly improve your well-being.

Achieving work-life balance as a solopreneur requires intentional effort and consistent boundary-setting. By creating a dedicated workspace, establishing a structured routine, setting boundaries with family and clients, and making time for self-care, you can build a sustainable balance between your personal and professional life. Remember, maintaining this balance is key to long-term success and well-being as a solopreneur, allowing you to thrive both in your business and in your personal life.

Understanding Taxes and Finances as a Solopreneur

Understanding taxes and managing finances as a solopreneur are critical components of running a successful business. Whether you're offering services, selling products, or working in a freelance capacity, knowing how to handle your financial responsibilities can help you avoid costly mistakes and ensure that your business remains profitable. This chapter will walk you through the key financial aspects of being a solopreneur, from managing income and expenses to navigating tax requirements and staying compliant with regulations.

Here's a comprehensive guide to help you understand taxes and finances as a solopreneur:

Separate Personal and Business Finances

One of the first steps in managing your finances as a solopreneur is to separate your personal and business finances. Mixing the two can lead to confusion, make it harder to track expenses, and complicate tax filing. Establishing clear boundaries between your business and personal accounts will help you stay organized and maintain accurate financial records.

Here's how to separate your finances:

Open a business bank account: If you're operating as a sole proprietor, you may not be legally required to have a separate bank account, but it's highly recommended. A business bank account allows you to track income, expenses, and profits more easily. If you have a registered business entity (e.g., LLC), a separate business account is often required by law.

Apply for a business credit card: Using a business credit card for all business-related purchases helps keep your transactions separate. It also allows you to build business credit, which can be helpful if you need to apply for business loans in the future.

Track income and expenses: Use accounting software, spreadsheets, or a bookkeeping service to record your business income and expenses regularly. This ensures that your records are accurate and up-to-date, making it easier to manage cash flow and prepare for tax season.

By separating your finances, you can avoid financial confusion and ensure you have a clear picture of your business's profitability.

Understand Your Tax Obligations

As a solopreneur, you are responsible for handling your own taxes. Unlike employees who have taxes automatically withheld from their paychecks, solopreneurs must calculate and pay taxes on their income themselves. Understanding the types of taxes you need to pay and how to stay compliant with tax laws is essential.

Here are the main types of taxes you'll need to be aware of:

Self-employment tax: Solopreneurs are required to pay self-employment tax, which covers Social Security and Medicare contributions. In 2024, the self-employment tax rate is 15.3% (12.4% for Social Security and 2.9% for Medicare). This tax is calculated based on your net income (profit) from your business.

Income tax: In addition to self-employment tax, you'll need to pay federal and state income taxes on your earnings. Your income tax rate will depend on your total income and the tax bracket you fall into. Keep in mind that many solopreneurs will need to make quarterly estimated tax payments to avoid penalties for underpayment.

Sales tax: If you sell physical products or certain digital goods and services, you may be required to collect sales tax from your customers. The rules for sales tax vary by state, so check the specific regulations in your location. Many e-commerce platforms offer tools that automatically calculate and collect sales tax based on where your customers are located.

Other business taxes: Depending on your business structure and location, you may also be subject to other taxes, such as franchise taxes or gross receipts taxes. If you operate as an LLC or corporation, additional taxes and fees may apply.

Calculate and Pay Estimated Taxes

Solopreneurs are generally required to pay estimated taxes throughout the year, rather than waiting until tax season to pay a lump sum. Estimated taxes are paid on a quarterly basis, covering your federal and state income taxes, as well as self-employment taxes. Failure to make these payments can result in penalties and interest charges.

Here's how to calculate and pay estimated taxes:

Estimate your taxable income: To calculate your estimated taxes, first estimate your expected income for the year. Subtract any business expenses to determine your net profit (taxable income).

Use IRS Form 1040-ES: The IRS provides Form 1040-ES, which includes instructions and worksheets to help you calculate your estimated tax payments. You'll need to consider both your income tax and self-employment tax when calculating the total amount.

Make quarterly payments: Estimated tax payments are due four times a year: April 15, June 15, September 15, and January 15 of the following year. You can make these payments electronically through the IRS's Electronic Federal Tax Payment System (EFTPS) or by mail.

Stay on top of state tax deadlines: In addition to federal estimated tax payments, you may need to make quarterly payments for state income taxes. Check your state's tax agency for deadlines and instructions on how to submit payments.

By making estimated tax payments on time, you can avoid penalties and ensure that you're meeting your tax obligations throughout the year.

Keep Track of Business Expenses

Tracking your business expenses is crucial for understanding your profitability and minimizing your tax liability. Many business expenses are tax-deductible, meaning they can reduce your taxable income and lower the amount of taxes you owe.

Here are common tax-deductible business expenses for solopreneurs:

Home office deduction: If you work from home, you may be eligible for the home office deduction. To qualify, your home office must be used exclusively and regularly for business purposes. You can either deduct a portion of your rent, mortgage, utilities, and insurance based on the square footage of your office, or use the simplified method of deducting $5 per square foot of office space (up to 300 square feet).

Business equipment and supplies: Any equipment or supplies you purchase for your business, such as a computer, printer, software, or office supplies, are tax-deductible. Keep receipts and records of these purchases for tax purposes.

Travel and meals: If you travel for business, you can deduct expenses such as airfare, lodging, car rentals, and meals. Meals are generally 50% deductible, as long as they are directly related to business activities.

Marketing and advertising: Any expenses related to marketing and promoting your business, such as website hosting, online ads, or business cards, can be deducted as business expenses.

Professional services: Fees paid to accountants, lawyers, consultants, or other professionals who provide services to your business are tax-deductible. These expenses help you run your business more effectively and can reduce your tax liability.

Health insurance premiums: If you're self-employed and pay for your own health insurance, you may be eligible to deduct the cost of premiums for yourself and your dependents. This deduction applies even if you don't itemize your deductions.

Tracking your business expenses consistently throughout the year makes tax filing easier and helps you take advantage of all the deductions available to you.

Choose the Right Business Structure for Tax Purposes

Your business structure has a significant impact on your taxes. Most solopreneurs operate as sole proprietors, but you may also choose to form a limited liability company (LLC) or corporation, depending on your goals and the tax implications.

Here's an overview of common business structures:

Sole proprietorship: The simplest and most common structure for solopreneurs, a sole proprietorship doesn't require formal registration, and your business income is reported on your personal tax return. You are responsible for paying self-employment taxes, and there's no legal distinction between you and your business.

LLC (Limited Liability Company): An LLC provides legal protection by separating your personal assets from your business liabilities. For tax purposes, an LLC can be treated as a sole proprietorship (if you're the only owner) or as a corporation. LLC owners can deduct business expenses and avoid double taxation, but they still need to pay self-employment taxes.

S Corporation: An S Corporation offers pass-through taxation, meaning the business's profits and losses are reported on the owner's personal tax return, avoiding double taxation. S Corporation owners can also pay themselves a salary and take distributions, which may reduce the amount of self-employment tax they owe.

C Corporation: A C Corporation is a separate legal entity that pays corporate income tax on its profits. Shareholders (owners) are also taxed on dividends they receive, which can result in double taxation. However, C Corporations can offer certain tax benefits, such as the ability to retain earnings within the company.

Choosing the right business structure depends on factors such as your income level, liability concerns, and tax goals. Consult a tax advisor or accountant to determine which structure is most advantageous for your situation.

Use Accounting Software or Hire a Professional

Managing your finances can be overwhelming, especially as your business grows. To stay organized and ensure accurate records, consider using accounting software or hiring a professional accountant to help you with bookkeeping, tax filing, and financial planning.

Here's how to streamline your financial management:

Accounting software: Tools like QuickBooks, FreshBooks, or Xero can help you manage your income, expenses, invoices, and taxes all in one place. These platforms often integrate with your bank accounts and payment processors, making it easy to track your finances in real time.

Hire a bookkeeper: If you prefer to focus on your business rather than managing finances, hiring a bookkeeper can help. A bookkeeper will handle day-to-day financial tasks, such as recording transactions, reconciling accounts, and preparing financial reports.

Work with an accountant: An accountant can provide valuable advice on tax strategies, help you with tax filing, and ensure that you're complying with tax laws. They can also assist with long-term financial planning, such as retirement savings, business expansion, and investments.

Using the right tools or professionals can save you time, reduce stress, and ensure that your finances are managed effectively.

Plan for Retirement and Savings

As a solopreneur, you don't have access to employer-sponsored retirement plans, so it's important to take control of your own retirement savings. Setting aside money for the future not only helps secure your financial well-being but also provides tax benefits.

Here are retirement savings options for solopreneurs:

SEP IRA (Simplified Employee Pension): A SEP IRA allows you to contribute up to 25% of your net self-employment earnings, with a maximum contribution limit of $66,000 in 2024. Contributions are tax-deductible, which reduces your taxable income for the year.

Solo 401(k): A Solo 401(k) is designed for self-employed individuals without employees. You can contribute both as an employee and employer, allowing you to save more for retirement. For 2024, you can contribute up to $22,500 as an employee, plus an additional 25% of your net earnings as an employer, for a total contribution of up to $66,000.

Traditional or Roth IRA: You can also contribute to a traditional IRA (which offers tax-deductible contributions) or a Roth IRA (which offers tax-free withdrawals in retirement). The contribution limit for both types of IRAs is $6,500 in 2024 ($7,500 if you're over 50).

Create an emergency fund: In addition to retirement savings, it's important to have an emergency fund to cover unexpected expenses or periods of slow business. Aim to save at least three to six months' worth of living expenses in a separate account.

Planning for retirement and savings ensures long-term financial stability and allows you to take advantage of tax-advantaged accounts to reduce your tax burden.

Understanding taxes and managing your finances as a solopreneur are essential for running a successful and sustainable business. By separating your personal and business finances, staying compliant with tax regulations, and planning for the future, you can avoid costly mistakes and ensure that your business remains financially healthy. Taking control of your finances not only provides peace of mind but also allows you to focus on growing your business and achieving your goals.

Why Solopreneurs Should Embrace Automation

Solopreneurs often wear multiple hats, managing everything from marketing and customer service to operations and finances. With so many responsibilities, it's easy to feel overwhelmed and stretched thin. This is where automation becomes a game-changer. By automating repetitive tasks and processes, solopreneurs can save time, improve efficiency, and focus on what really matters—growing their business.

Embracing automation doesn't mean you're losing the personal touch. Instead, it allows you to streamline your workflow, reduce errors, and deliver a better customer experience. In this chapter, we'll explore why solopreneurs should embrace automation and how it can transform your business.

Save Time on Repetitive Tasks

As a solopreneur, your time is one of your most valuable resources. However, many day-to-day tasks, such as sending emails, managing social media, and handling administrative duties, can eat up hours of your workday. Automation allows you to offload these repetitive tasks, freeing up time for more strategic and creative work.

Here's how automation saves time:

Email marketing automation: Tools like Mailchimp, ActiveCampaign, or ConvertKit allow you to automate your email campaigns, welcome sequences, and follow-up messages. Instead of manually sending emails to each new subscriber, you can set up automated workflows that nurture leads, promote products, and engage customers.

Social media scheduling: Automating your social media posts with tools like Buffer, Hootsuite, or Later can save you hours each week. You can batch-create content and schedule it in advance, ensuring a consistent online presence without constantly managing your accounts.

Task management: Automating repetitive tasks like data entry, scheduling, and invoicing with platforms like Zapier, Trello, or Asana allows you to focus on higher-value activities. For example, you can automate invoice generation or set up automatic reminders for deadlines.

By automating time-consuming tasks, solopreneurs can reclaim valuable hours in their day and invest that time in growing their business, developing new products, or improving customer relationships.

Improve Efficiency and Productivity

Automation improves efficiency by eliminating the need for manual intervention in repetitive tasks. This not only reduces the likelihood of errors but also increases productivity by allowing you to focus on more complex and meaningful work. With automation, you can complete tasks faster and more accurately, which leads to higher output without increasing your workload.

Here's how automation improves efficiency:

Streamlined workflows: Automation tools can create seamless workflows that move tasks from one step to the next without requiring your constant attention. For instance, you can set up workflows where new customer inquiries trigger an automatic email response, schedule follow-up reminders, and update your CRM system—all without manual input.

Data accuracy: Automation reduces the risk of human error in tasks such as data entry, reporting, or financial management. For example, accounting software like QuickBooks or Xero can automate bookkeeping tasks, such as reconciling bank accounts, categorizing expenses, and generating financial reports. This minimizes errors and ensures that your financial data is accurate.

Faster decision-making: Automation tools can provide real-time insights and analytics, helping you make informed decisions faster. Whether it's tracking customer behavior, website analytics, or sales performance, having access to up-to-date data allows you to adjust your strategy on the fly and respond to trends quickly.

By automating routine tasks, solopreneurs can boost efficiency, increase productivity, and focus on the aspects of their business that require creativity and strategic thinking.

Deliver a Better Customer Experience

Providing a great customer experience is key to building loyalty and growing your business. However, managing customer interactions manually can be time-consuming and prone to delays. Automation can help solopreneurs deliver faster, more personalized service while maintaining high-quality customer engagement.

Here's how automation enhances the customer experience:

Faster response times: With automation, you can set up instant responses to customer inquiries. For example, automated chatbots or email autoresponders can provide quick answers to common questions or let customers know when they can expect a more detailed response. This ensures that customers aren't left waiting and feel acknowledged right away.

Personalized communication: Automation tools allow you to personalize your communication based on customer behavior. For instance, you can set up email campaigns that send personalized product recommendations, exclusive offers, or birthday greetings to your customers based on their purchase history or preferences. This helps build stronger relationships and increases customer retention.

Efficient onboarding: If you offer digital products, courses, or services, automation can streamline the onboarding process for new customers. You can create automated workflows that deliver welcome emails, product tutorials, and next steps to guide new customers through their journey.

Consistent follow-up: One of the most common challenges solopreneurs face is keeping up with customer follow-ups. Automation tools can schedule follow-up emails or messages at the right intervals, ensuring that you stay connected with leads and customers without having to remember each individual task.

By automating customer interactions, solopreneurs can deliver a more responsive, personalized, and consistent experience, which in turn builds trust and encourages repeat business.

Scale Your Business More Easily

Automation is an essential tool for solopreneurs looking to scale their business. As your business grows, managing every task manually becomes increasingly difficult. By automating processes, you can handle more customers, orders, or projects without adding additional staff or resources.

Here's how automation supports business growth:

Handle higher volumes: With automation in place, solopreneurs can manage a higher volume of orders, clients, or projects without sacrificing quality or efficiency. For example, an e-commerce business can automate order processing, payment confirmations, and shipping notifications, allowing you to fulfill more orders in less time.

Optimize marketing efforts: Automating marketing campaigns allows you to reach a larger audience without the need for constant oversight. For instance, you can set up automated email campaigns that nurture leads over time, or use retargeting ads that automatically show your products to customers who have visited your website but haven't made a purchase.

Streamline project management: Solopreneurs who manage multiple clients or projects can use project management tools like Monday.com, ClickUp, or Asana to automate task assignments, deadlines, and progress tracking. This ensures that projects move forward efficiently and deadlines are met, even as your workload increases.

Reduce administrative overhead: As your business scales, administrative tasks can quickly pile up. Automating these tasks—such as invoicing, payroll, and tax reporting—frees up your time and allows you to focus on strategic activities that drive growth.

Automation allows solopreneurs to grow their business without being bogged down by administrative tasks or stretched too thin by increased demand. By automating key processes, you can scale your business more sustainably and efficiently.

REDUCE COSTS AND INCREASE Profitability

Automation can help solopreneurs reduce operating costs and increase profitability. By streamlining workflows, reducing the need for manual labor, and minimizing errors, automation enables you to run your business more cost-effectively. This, in turn, frees up resources that can be reinvested into growth and innovation.

Here's how automation reduces costs:

Lower labor costs: Automating repetitive tasks eliminates the need for hiring additional staff to handle these activities. For example, instead of hiring an assistant to manage customer support emails, you can use chatbots or automated email responders to handle common inquiries.

Reduce human error: Mistakes in tasks like data entry, financial reporting, or inventory management can be costly. Automation minimizes the risk of errors, reducing the potential for financial losses, missed deadlines, or dissatisfied customers.

Optimize resource allocation: By automating administrative tasks, solopreneurs can focus their time and energy on high-value activities, such as business development, product creation, or client engagement. This increases overall productivity and maximizes the return on investment for your time and resources.

Track financial performance: Accounting software and financial tools can automate expense tracking, invoicing, and tax calculations, helping you better understand your cash flow and profitability. Automation also allows you to identify cost-saving opportunities, such as reducing overhead or optimizing pricing strategies. By embracing automation, solopreneurs can reduce overhead, improve profitability, and run their business more efficiently.

Maintain Consistency and Reliability

Consistency is key to building a successful business, and automation helps solopreneurs deliver consistent results every time. Whether it's responding to customer inquiries, posting on social media, or processing orders, automation ensures that tasks are completed on time and according to plan.

Here's how automation improves consistency:

Regular content posting: Social media scheduling tools ensure that you post content consistently, even when you're busy with other tasks. A steady posting schedule helps you maintain visibility and engagement with your audience.

Automated billing and payments: Automating invoicing and payment collection ensures that you send invoices on time and follow up on late payments without manual intervention. This helps maintain a steady cash flow and reduces the risk of missed payments.

Consistent workflows: Automating workflows ensures that tasks are completed in the correct order and on schedule. For example, if you have a set process for onboarding new clients, automation ensures that each client receives the same high-quality experience, no matter how busy you are.

Scheduled reminders and follow-ups: Automation tools can send reminders for tasks like project deadlines, meetings, or contract renewals. This helps ensure that nothing slips through the cracks, allowing you to stay on top of your commitments and maintain a professional reputation. Consistency is essential for building trust with customers and clients, and automation helps solopreneurs deliver reliable results, even when managing multiple tasks or projects.

Gain Insights and Data-Driven Decision Making

Automation tools often come with built-in analytics and reporting features that provide valuable insights into your business operations. These insights allow you to make data-driven decisions, optimize your processes, and identify areas for improvement.

Here's how automation supports data-driven decision-making:

Track performance metrics: Many automation tools provide real-time data on key performance indicators (KPIs) such as sales, website traffic, customer engagement, and conversion rates. By analyzing these metrics, you can identify trends, measure the success of marketing campaigns, and adjust your strategy accordingly.

Monitor customer behavior: Automation tools can track how customers interact with your website, emails, or products, giving you insights into their preferences and behavior. For example, you can use email marketing software to see which emails are opened the most or which links are clicked, allowing you to refine your content and offers.

Identify bottlenecks: Automation allows you to track the progress of tasks and workflows, helping you identify bottlenecks or inefficiencies. For instance, if certain tasks take longer than expected or orders are frequently delayed, you can use automation data to pinpoint the cause and implement improvements.

Optimize marketing efforts: Automated marketing tools provide detailed analytics on campaign performance, helping you understand which channels and strategies are driving the most sales. This enables you to allocate your marketing budget more effectively and focus on high-impact activities.By using automation to gather data and insights, solopreneurs can make more informed decisions, optimize their operations, and drive business growth. Automation is a powerful tool that can transform the way solopreneurs run their businesses. By automating repetitive tasks, improving efficiency, enhancing customer experiences, and providing data-driven insights, solopreneurs can save time, reduce costs, and focus on growing their business. Embracing automation allows you to scale more easily, maintain consistency, and achieve a better work-life balance, ultimately leading to long-term success and sustainability.

Outsourcing vs. Doing It All Yourself: What's Right for You?

As a solopreneur, you're used to wearing many hats, from marketing and sales to customer service, accounting, and everything in between. While managing all aspects of your business may seem cost-effective initially, it can quickly lead to burnout, inefficiencies, and missed opportunities for growth. The key to scaling your business and maintaining work-life balance often lies in deciding when to outsource tasks and when to handle them yourself.

In this chapter, we'll explore the pros and cons of outsourcing versus doing it all yourself, helping you determine what's right for your solopreneur journey. Understanding when to delegate tasks to others can help you optimize your time, improve efficiency, and focus on what you do best.

The Benefits of Doing It All Yourself

For many solopreneurs, the desire to maintain control and keep costs low leads to the decision to do everything themselves. There are several advantages to this approach, particularly when you're just starting out or working with a limited budget.

Here's why doing it all yourself can be beneficial:

Complete control over your business: When you manage every aspect of your business, you have full control over every decision, task, and outcome. You can ensure that your brand is represented exactly as you envision it, and you don't have to rely on others to meet your standards.

Cost savings: By handling everything on your own, you avoid the expense of hiring freelancers, contractors, or agencies. This can be especially important when your business is in its early stages and you're operating on a tight budget. Every dollar saved can be reinvested in other areas of growth.

Learning new skills: Managing all aspects of your business forces you to learn a wide range of skills, from web design to bookkeeping. These skills can be valuable long-term, as they give you a better understanding of your business and make you more self-sufficient.

Flexibility and agility: When you're the only one managing your business, you can quickly adapt to changes, pivot strategies, and make decisions without having to consult with a team or wait for others to act. This level of agility can be advantageous in fast-moving industries.

While doing it all yourself has its advantages, it's important to recognize the potential downsides, especially as your business grows. Managing every task can lead to exhaustion, inefficiency, and missed growth opportunities.

THE DRAWBACKS OF DOING It All Yourself

Although solopreneurs may feel capable of managing everything on their own, the reality is that handling all tasks yourself can quickly become overwhelming. As your business expands, it becomes harder to manage every aspect effectively, and the quality of your work may suffer.

Here are some drawbacks to doing it all yourself:

Time constraints: As a solopreneur, your time is limited. When you're responsible for every task, you can quickly find yourself stretched too thin, leaving little time for strategic planning, creativity, or personal time. Tasks like bookkeeping, customer support, and administrative work can consume hours of your day, preventing you from focusing on core business activities.

Burnout and stress: Juggling multiple roles and responsibilities can lead to burnout. Constantly working long hours, managing deadlines, and switching between tasks can take a toll on your mental and physical well-being, ultimately affecting your productivity and motivation.

Lack of expertise: While learning new skills is valuable, there are certain areas where outsourcing to experts can produce better results. For example, tasks like website design, legal compliance, or digital marketing may require specialized knowledge that you don't have. Trying to manage these tasks yourself can lead to mistakes and suboptimal results.

Missed growth opportunities: By focusing on day-to-day operations, you may miss out on opportunities to grow your business. Tasks that could be delegated to others, such as social media management or content creation, can take up valuable time that could be spent on business development, product innovation, or building client relationships.

Recognizing these drawbacks is the first step in understanding when outsourcing may be the right solution for your business.

The Benefits of Outsourcing

Outsourcing is the process of hiring external contractors, freelancers, or agencies to handle specific tasks or projects. For solopreneurs, outsourcing can be a powerful strategy for scaling your business, improving efficiency, and maintaining work-life balance.

Here's why outsourcing can be beneficial:

Focus on core competencies: Outsourcing allows you to focus on the aspects of your business that you're passionate about and excel at, whether that's product development, sales, or client relations. By delegating non-core tasks to others, you free up time to focus on activities that drive growth and align with your strengths.

Access to specialized expertise: Outsourcing gives you access to experts in various fields, such as marketing, design, legal, or financial management. Instead of spending hours learning new skills, you can hire professionals who already have the knowledge and experience to deliver high-quality results.

Increased efficiency: By outsourcing tasks to specialists, you can improve efficiency and productivity. For example, a professional web designer can build a website more quickly and effectively than if you were to attempt it yourself. This allows you to launch projects faster and with better results.

Scalability: As your business grows, outsourcing allows you to scale your operations without hiring full-time employees. You can bring on freelancers or contractors as needed, without the long-term commitment of hiring permanent staff. This flexibility enables you to handle increased workloads during busy periods or large projects without overwhelming yourself.

Reduced stress and burnout: Delegating time-consuming tasks to others can reduce your workload and prevent burnout. By outsourcing tasks like customer support, bookkeeping, or content creation, you can maintain a healthier work-life balance and avoid feeling overworked.

Outsourcing offers solopreneurs the opportunity to grow their business more efficiently, access expert skills, and maintain balance—without the need to do everything themselves.

The Drawbacks of Outsourcing

While outsourcing can be highly beneficial, it's important to be aware of the potential drawbacks and challenges that come with it. Outsourcing isn't always the right solution for every task, and it requires careful management to ensure success.

Here are some potential downsides to outsourcing:

Loss of control: When you outsource tasks, you're handing over control to someone else. This can be challenging for solopreneurs who are used to managing every detail of their business. Ensuring that the quality of work meets your standards may require more oversight and communication than expected.

Cost considerations: While outsourcing can save time, it often comes with a financial cost. Hiring freelancers or agencies can be expensive, especially for specialized tasks. Solopreneurs need to weigh the cost of outsourcing against the potential return on investment (ROI).

Finding the right fit: Not all freelancers or agencies are created equal. Finding the right person or team to work with can take time, and there's a risk that the quality of work may not meet your expectations. It's important to thoroughly vet potential partners, check their portfolios, and establish clear expectations before outsourcing.

Communication challenges: Working with external contractors can sometimes lead to communication challenges, especially if they're located in different time zones or have different working styles. Clear communication is essential to ensure that tasks are completed on time and to your satisfaction.

Potential for inconsistent quality: When outsourcing to freelancers, there's always the risk that the quality of work may be inconsistent. While some freelancers may deliver exceptional results, others may not meet your standards. It's important to set clear expectations, provide feedback, and build long-term relationships with reliable contractors.

Despite these potential challenges, many solopreneurs find that the benefits of outsourcing outweigh the risks, especially when it allows them to focus on what they do best and grow their business.

When to Consider Outsourcing

Deciding when to outsource is a key factor in optimizing your business operations. As a solopreneur, knowing which tasks to delegate and which to handle yourself can help you strike the right balance between control and efficiency.

Here are some signs that it may be time to consider outsourcing:

You're feeling overwhelmed: If you're constantly stressed, overworked, or struggling to keep up with tasks, it's a clear sign that you need help. Outsourcing can relieve the pressure and give you more time to focus on important tasks that only you can handle.

You're spending too much time on non-core tasks: If you're spending more time on administrative tasks, customer support, or technical work than on growing your business, it's time to delegate. Outsourcing these tasks frees you up to focus on strategic activities like marketing, product development, or sales.

You lack the necessary expertise: If there are areas of your business that require specialized skills—such as web development, legal compliance, or SEO—you may benefit from outsourcing to professionals who can deliver better results. Trying to manage these tasks on your own may lead to costly mistakes.

Your business is growing: As your business grows, you may find it difficult to manage everything yourself. Outsourcing allows you to scale your operations and handle increased demand without sacrificing quality or customer service.

You want to improve efficiency: If you're looking for ways to streamline your workflow and increase efficiency, outsourcing can help. Tasks like bookkeeping, social media management, or content creation can be outsourced to experts who can complete them faster and with higher quality than if you were to do them yourself.

By recognizing these signs, you can determine when it's the right time to outsource and which tasks to delegate.

What to Outsource

Not all tasks need to be outsourced, and some are better handled by you, especially those that directly impact your brand or customer relationships. However, there are certain tasks that solopreneurs commonly outsource to free up time and improve efficiency.

Here are some tasks to consider outsourcing:

Administrative tasks: Virtual assistants (VAs) can handle administrative tasks like email management, scheduling, data entry, and customer support. Outsourcing these tasks allows you to focus on high-value activities.

Marketing and social media: Many solopreneurs outsource marketing tasks, such as social media management, content creation, email marketing, and paid advertising. This helps ensure that your brand stays visible without you having to manage every post or campaign.

Website design and maintenance: If you don't have web development skills, outsourcing website design and maintenance to a professional can save you time and ensure that your site is optimized for performance and user experience.

Accounting and bookkeeping: Outsourcing bookkeeping and accounting tasks to a professional ensures that your finances are accurate and compliant with tax regulations. An accountant can help with tax planning, financial reporting, and cash flow management.

Graphic design and branding: Creating a strong brand identity often requires professional graphic design services. Outsourcing logo design, business card creation, or product packaging to a designer ensures a cohesive and professional look for your brand.

Legal services: Legal tasks, such as drafting contracts, trademarks, or handling business registrations, are best left to professionals. Outsourcing legal services helps you avoid costly mistakes and ensures that your business is legally protected.

By outsourcing these tasks, you can focus on growing your business and delivering value to your customers.

What to Handle Yourself

While outsourcing is an effective strategy, there are certain tasks that solopreneurs should handle themselves, especially those that directly impact your brand, business development, or customer relationships.

HERE'S WHAT YOU SHOULD consider handling yourself:

Business strategy and decision-making: As the business owner, you're responsible for setting the vision, strategy, and direction of your company. Major decisions about growth, partnerships, and product development should remain under your control.

Client relationships: Building and maintaining strong relationships with your clients is essential for long-term success. While you can outsource customer support, direct communication with key clients should be handled personally.

Product or service development: If your business revolves around your expertise or creativity, it's important to stay involved in product or service development. For example, if you're a solopreneur selling online courses, coaching services, or handmade products, your personal touch is a key part of the value you offer.

Brand voice and messaging: Your brand's voice and messaging are critical to how you connect with your audience. While you can outsource content creation, you should oversee how your brand is represented in marketing materials, website copy, and social media.

By keeping control of these core aspects, you can ensure that your business stays true to your vision and delivers the value that sets you apart from competitors.

Deciding whether to outsource or handle tasks yourself is a critical decision for solopreneurs. While doing everything yourself offers control and cost savings, it can also lead to burnout, inefficiency, and missed opportunities. On the other hand, outsourcing can improve efficiency, give you access to specialized expertise, and free up time for growth, but it requires careful management and financial investment.

The key is to find the right balance. Start by outsourcing tasks that are time-consuming or outside your area of expertise, and focus on the aspects of your business that require your personal touch. As your business grows, outsourcing becomes an essential strategy for scaling while maintaining a healthy work-life balance. By strategically delegating tasks, you can optimize your operations, stay focused on your core strengths, and position your solopreneur business for long-term success.

Navigating the Challenges of Solopreneurship

Solopreneurship offers the freedom and flexibility to build a business on your terms, but it also comes with its fair share of challenges. Without a team to rely on, solopreneurs must tackle a variety of hurdles, from managing time effectively and wearing multiple hats to dealing with isolation and uncertainty. Navigating these challenges requires resilience, creativity, and strategic thinking.

In this chapter, we'll explore some of the most common challenges solopreneurs face and provide practical strategies for overcoming them. By understanding these obstacles and learning how to manage them, you can build a more sustainable and successful business.

Time Management and Overwhelm

One of the biggest challenges solopreneurs face is managing time effectively. Without the structure of a traditional job or a team to delegate tasks to, it's easy to feel overwhelmed by the sheer volume of responsibilities. From handling client work and marketing to managing finances and customer support, solopreneurs must juggle many tasks while trying to stay focused on growing their business.

Here's how to manage time and avoid overwhelm:

Prioritize your tasks: Not all tasks are created equal. Use a system like the Eisenhower Matrix to categorize tasks based on their urgency and importance. Focus on high-priority tasks that directly contribute to your business growth or client satisfaction, and delegate or eliminate low-priority activities.

Set boundaries: It's easy to blur the lines between work and personal life when you're a solopreneur. Set specific working hours and stick to them. Avoid the temptation to work late into the night or on weekends, as this can lead to burnout. Create a clear boundary between work time and personal time to maintain balance.

Use time management tools: Apps like Trello, Asana, or Todoist can help you stay organized and manage your tasks more efficiently. These tools allow you to break down larger projects into manageable steps, set deadlines, and track your progress.

Learn to say no: Solopreneurs often feel pressure to take on every opportunity or client request, but this can lead to over-commitment and burnout. Learn to say no to tasks or projects that don't align with your goals or capacity, and focus on what truly matters.

By prioritizing your tasks, setting boundaries, and using time management tools, you can manage your workload more effectively and reduce feelings of overwhelm.

WEARING MULTIPLE HATS

As a solopreneur, you're responsible for every aspect of your business. One day you might be working on marketing, the next day handling customer inquiries, and the day after that managing finances. While this gives you full control, it also requires you to constantly switch between different roles, which can be mentally exhausting and inefficient.

Here's how to manage wearing multiple hats:

Batch your tasks: Instead of jumping from one task to another throughout the day, try batching similar tasks together. For example, dedicate one morning to marketing activities, one afternoon to administrative work, and another block of time for client work. Batching tasks reduces context switching and helps you stay focused.

Automate where possible: Automate repetitive tasks like email responses, invoicing, or social media scheduling. Tools like Zapier, Mailchimp, or Buffer can help you streamline processes, freeing up more time for high-value work.

Outsource specialized tasks: If you find that certain tasks are taking up too much time or require skills you don't have, consider outsourcing them. Hiring a virtual assistant, graphic designer, or accountant can help lighten your load and ensure tasks are completed efficiently.

Create systems and processes: Establish clear systems and workflows for recurring tasks. This helps you stay organized and reduces the time spent figuring out how to approach each new task. Document your processes so that if you decide to outsource or bring on help in the future, you can easily delegate tasks.

By batching tasks, automating processes, and creating clear systems, you can manage your various roles more efficiently and avoid feeling pulled in too many directions.

Dealing with Isolation

Running a business on your own can be a lonely experience, especially if you're working from home or in a remote location. Unlike traditional office environments, where you can interact with colleagues and share ideas, solopreneurs often work in isolation. This lack of social interaction can lead to feelings of loneliness and disconnection.

Here's how to overcome isolation as a solopreneur:

Join online communities: There are many online communities and forums where solopreneurs and entrepreneurs gather to share advice, support, and inspiration. Joining groups on platforms like LinkedIn, Facebook, or Reddit can provide you with a sense of camaraderie and a network of like-minded individuals.

Attend networking events: In-person or virtual networking events, conferences, and workshops provide opportunities to meet other business owners, learn new skills, and exchange ideas. Even if you work remotely, making an effort to connect with others in your industry can combat feelings of isolation.

Find an accountability partner or mentor: Partnering with another solopreneur or entrepreneur for accountability can provide motivation and support. A mentor or coach can also offer guidance and a sounding board for your ideas. Regular check-ins with someone who understands your challenges can make a big difference in staying motivated and focused.

Work from coworking spaces: If you're feeling isolated working from home, consider spending a few days a week at a coworking space. These spaces provide opportunities to interact with other professionals, share ideas, and break up the monotony of working alone.

By actively seeking out social interactions and building a network of supportive peers, you can mitigate the feelings of isolation that often come with solopreneurship.

Handling Financial Uncertainty

One of the most significant challenges of solopreneurship is managing the financial ups and downs. Unlike traditional employment, where you receive a steady paycheck, solopreneurs often experience fluctuating income, especially in the early stages of business. This unpredictability can lead to stress and uncertainty about the future.

Here's how to manage financial uncertainty:

Create a financial buffer: Build an emergency fund with enough savings to cover at least three to six months of living expenses. Having a financial cushion provides peace of mind during slower months or unexpected expenses, allowing you to focus on growing your business without the constant pressure of making ends meet.

Diversify your income streams: Relying on a single client or income source can be risky. Consider diversifying your revenue streams by offering additional services, launching digital products, or building passive income through affiliate marketing, online courses, or eBooks. This reduces your dependence on one source of income and helps stabilize your cash flow.

Track your finances: Use accounting software like QuickBooks, FreshBooks, or Xero to track your income, expenses, and cash flow. Keeping a close eye on your finances allows you to make informed decisions about spending, saving, and investing in your business.

Set a budget: Establish a clear budget for both your personal and business finances. Stick to your budget to avoid overspending during profitable months, and prioritize saving and reinvesting in your business for long-term stability.

Plan for slow periods: Solopreneurs often experience slow periods, especially in industries with seasonal fluctuations. Anticipate these slower months by setting aside extra income during busier times. You can also use slow periods to focus on marketing, product development, or networking to prepare for future growth.

By building a financial buffer, diversifying your income, and staying on top of your finances, you can navigate the financial uncertainties of solopreneurship with more confidence.

Managing Self-Doubt and Imposter Syndrome

Imposter syndrome—the feeling of not being good enough or not deserving your success—is a common challenge among solopreneurs. Without a team or boss to provide validation, many solopreneurs struggle with self-doubt, questioning their abilities and worth.

Here's how to overcome self-doubt and imposter syndrome:

Acknowledge your achievements: Take time to recognize your accomplishments, no matter how small. Keep a journal or list of milestones, client testimonials, and positive feedback to remind yourself of the value you bring to your business and customers.

Focus on continuous learning: Embrace a growth mindset by recognizing that you don't have to know everything right away. Focus on learning and improving rather than achieving perfection. Seek out opportunities for professional development, such as courses, workshops, or mentorship, to build your skills and confidence.

Reframe negative thoughts: When self-doubt creeps in, challenge those thoughts by reframing them in a more positive light. Instead of thinking, "I'm not qualified," remind yourself, "I'm constantly learning and improving, and I've already achieved a lot." Changing your inner dialogue can help combat imposter syndrome.

Surround yourself with supportive people: Build a network of supportive peers, mentors, or fellow solopreneurs who understand your challenges and can offer encouragement. Surrounding yourself with positive influences can help boost your confidence and provide perspective when self-doubt arises.

Celebrate progress, not perfection: Solopreneurship is a journey, and progress is often more important than perfection. Celebrate your growth, milestones, and improvements along the way, even if things aren't perfect. Recognize that everyone faces challenges, and perfection is rarely attainable.

By focusing on your achievements, seeking continuous learning, and surrounding yourself with supportive individuals, you can overcome self-doubt and build confidence in your abilities as a solopreneur.

Staying Motivated and Focused

Without a boss or team to keep you accountable, staying motivated and focused as a solopreneur can be challenging. Distractions, procrastination, and a lack of structure can lead to missed deadlines or a lack of progress on your business goals.

Here's how to stay motivated and focused as a solopreneur:

Staying Motivated and Focused

Without a boss or a team to hold you accountable, staying motivated and focused can be one of the most significant challenges of solopreneurship. Distractions, procrastination, and the lack of a structured environment can slow down your progress and impact your business's growth. However, with the right mindset and strategies, you can maintain motivation and keep your business moving forward.

Here's how to stay motivated and focused as a solopreneur:

Set clear goals: Having clear, actionable goals helps you stay focused and gives you a sense of direction. Break down your larger business objectives into smaller, manageable tasks that you can work on daily or weekly. Setting both short-term and long-term goals helps keep you motivated as you see measurable progress over time.

Create a routine: Establish a daily routine that includes dedicated work hours, breaks, and time for personal activities. A consistent routine helps structure your day and reduces the temptation to procrastinate. Include a morning ritual that sets a positive tone for your workday, whether it's meditation, exercise, or journaling.

Use productivity techniques: Techniques like the Pomodoro Technique (working in focused 25-minute intervals followed by short breaks) or time blocking (scheduling specific blocks of time for different tasks) can help you stay focused and productive. Experiment with different productivity methods to find what works best for you.

Limit distractions: Identify the distractions that commonly derail your focus and take steps to minimize them. For example, if social media distracts you, use apps like Focus@Will or website blockers like Freedom to stay focused during work hours. Designate specific times during the day for checking emails or engaging on social media.

Reward yourself: To stay motivated, reward yourself when you accomplish tasks or reach milestones. These rewards can be as simple as taking a walk, having a special treat, or enjoying a break. Positive reinforcement helps keep you motivated and makes working towards goals more enjoyable.

Visualize your success: Visualization is a powerful technique for staying motivated. Take a few moments each day to visualize your long-term success, whether it's growing your business, achieving financial freedom, or reaching a personal goal. This can help you stay focused on the bigger picture and remind you why you started your business in the first place.

Stay connected with your "why": Reconnect with the reasons you became a solopreneur. Whether it's the desire for freedom, passion for your work, or the goal of creating something meaningful, keeping your "why" at the forefront of your mind can reignite your motivation when things get tough.

By setting clear goals, establishing a routine, and staying connected to your purpose, you can maintain motivation and focus as you navigate the ups and downs of solopreneurship.

Managing Uncertainty and Risk

Solopreneurship often involves navigating uncertain terrain, with no guaranteed income or security like traditional employment offers. Financial instability, market fluctuations, and evolving customer demands can create a sense of unpredictability. Learning to manage uncertainty and embrace risk is a crucial part of the solopreneur journey.

Here's how to manage uncertainty and take calculated risks:

Embrace a growth mindset: Having a growth mindset means viewing challenges and setbacks as opportunities for learning and improvement rather than failures. By adopting this mindset, you can approach uncertainty with curiosity and resilience, knowing that each experience contributes to your growth as a business owner.

Prepare for risks: While risk is an inherent part of business, you can mitigate its impact by preparing for it. Conduct thorough research before launching new products, entering new markets, or making major investments. Assess the potential risks and rewards of each decision, and have contingency plans in place in case things don't go as expected.

Diversify your income: Relying on a single income stream can increase your vulnerability to market changes or client loss. Diversifying your revenue streams by offering multiple products, services, or passive income opportunities can create more stability and reduce financial risk.

Build an emergency fund: Financial uncertainty is a common challenge for solopreneurs, especially during slow periods. Having an emergency fund that covers three to six months of living and business expenses can provide peace of mind and reduce stress during lean times.

Take calculated risks: While avoiding all risk may seem like a safe approach, solopreneurs who take calculated risks often see the greatest growth. Weigh the potential benefits against the risks, and trust your instincts when it comes to making strategic decisions. Remember, many successful solopreneurs have taken risks that led to breakthroughs in their business.

Stay adaptable: The ability to pivot and adapt to changing circumstances is critical for navigating uncertainty. Stay open to new opportunities, and be willing to shift your approach if needed. For example, if one marketing strategy isn't yielding results, try a new platform or campaign. Adaptability ensures that you're ready to face whatever challenges come your way.

By embracing a growth mindset, preparing for risks, and staying adaptable, you can navigate uncertainty and turn challenges into opportunities for growth.

Celebrating Small Wins

Solopreneurs often focus on the big picture and long-term success, but celebrating small wins along the way is just as important. Recognizing your progress and achievements, no matter how minor, keeps you motivated, boosts morale, and reinforces your commitment to your business.

Here's how to celebrate small wins as a solopreneur:

Acknowledge daily progress: Take a few moments at the end of each day to reflect on what you accomplished, even if it's as simple as sending an important email or finishing a task on your to-do list. Acknowledging daily progress helps you see the forward momentum, even on days when it feels like things aren't moving fast enough.

Track milestones: Whether you're launching a new product, reaching a revenue target, or gaining your first 100 email subscribers, keep track of milestones and celebrate them. Celebrating these milestones gives you a sense of accomplishment and reminds you of how far you've come.

Reward yourself: Rewarding yourself for achieving goals, both big and small, helps keep you motivated. The reward doesn't have to be extravagant—it could be taking a day off, enjoying a favorite meal, or indulging in a relaxing activity. Rewards create positive reinforcement and make the journey of solopreneurship more enjoyable.

Share your wins: Solopreneurship can sometimes feel like a solitary journey, but sharing your wins with others—whether it's friends, family, or an online community—can enhance the celebration. You'll receive support, encouragement, and validation, which helps reinforce your sense of achievement.

Focus on progress, not perfection: Celebrate your progress, even if things aren't perfect. Solopreneurship is a learning journey, and each step forward is worth recognizing. Celebrate the fact that you're consistently moving closer to your goals, and appreciate the effort you put into your business.

By celebrating small wins and taking time to acknowledge your progress, you can maintain a positive mindset and stay motivated through the challenges of solopreneurship. Navigating the challenges of solopreneurship requires a mix of resilience, adaptability, and strategic planning. From managing time and juggling multiple responsibilities to dealing with isolation and financial uncertainty, solopreneurs face a unique set of hurdles. However, by developing effective time management strategies, embracing outsourcing when needed, and fostering a growth mindset, you can overcome these challenges and build a sustainable, successful business. By staying connected to your purpose, celebrating small wins, and seeking support from a community of like-minded entrepreneurs, you'll be better equipped to navigate the highs and lows of solopreneurship. Ultimately, the journey of building your business is as rewarding as the destination, and with the right approach, you can thrive as a solopreneur in today's dynamic business landscape.

Building Resilience: How to Handle Solopreneur Stress

Building resilience is crucial for solopreneurs, who often face high levels of stress due to the pressures of managing every aspect of their business. Stress can stem from the uncertainty of income, the challenge of juggling multiple responsibilities, and the isolation that often comes with running a business alone. Learning how to handle stress and build resilience will not only help you navigate tough times but also ensure your long-term success and well-being as a solopreneur.

In this chapter, we'll explore strategies for managing stress, cultivating resilience, and maintaining balance as you navigate the highs and lows of solopreneurship.

Recognize the Sources of Stress

The first step in managing solopreneur stress is to recognize its sources. Stress can come from various areas of your business, and identifying these stressors is key to developing strategies to manage them.

Common sources of stress for solopreneurs include:

Financial uncertainty: The inconsistency of income is one of the biggest stressors for solopreneurs. There may be periods of high revenue followed by slower months, which can create anxiety about covering expenses or maintaining a steady cash flow.

Overwork and burnout: Solopreneurs often work long hours and wear multiple hats, leading to exhaustion and burnout. Trying to manage everything yourself can feel overwhelming and lead to mental and physical fatigue.

Client demands and deadlines: Managing client expectations, meeting deadlines, and handling difficult clients can create significant stress, especially if you're juggling multiple projects simultaneously.

Isolation: Many solopreneurs work alone, which can lead to feelings of loneliness and isolation. Without a support network or team, you may feel disconnected or lack someone to share ideas and challenges with.

Fear of failure: The pressure to succeed, especially when you're the sole person responsible for your business, can create constant stress. Fear of failure or making mistakes can lead to anxiety and self-doubt.

Once you identify the specific sources of stress in your business, you can begin to implement strategies to manage and reduce them.

Prioritize Self-Care

Self-care is one of the most important aspects of managing stress and building resilience. Taking care of your physical, mental, and emotional health allows you to stay energized, focused, and better equipped to handle challenges.

Here's how to prioritize self-care as a solopreneur:

Establish boundaries: Set clear boundaries between your work and personal life. Designate specific work hours, and avoid working late into the night or on weekends. Give yourself time to rest and recharge, even if it's just a few hours of downtime each day.

Get enough sleep: Lack of sleep can exacerbate stress and reduce your ability to handle challenges effectively. Aim for seven to nine hours of sleep each night to maintain your energy and focus. Creating a bedtime routine, such as turning off screens and relaxing before bed, can help you sleep better.

Exercise regularly: Physical activity is one of the most effective ways to reduce stress and improve mood. Whether it's walking, running, yoga, or strength training, find an exercise routine that you enjoy and can incorporate into your schedule. Exercise not only helps relieve stress but also boosts your overall well-being.

Practice mindfulness or meditation: Mindfulness and meditation can help reduce stress and improve your ability to stay present and focused. Take a few minutes each day to meditate, practice deep breathing, or engage in mindful activities like journaling. These practices help clear your mind and improve your emotional resilience.

Eat a balanced diet: What you eat can have a direct impact on your stress levels and energy. Eating a balanced diet that includes whole grains, fruits, vegetables, and lean proteins helps fuel your body and mind, allowing you to handle stress more effectively.

By prioritizing self-care, you'll have more energy, clarity, and resilience to face the challenges of solopreneurship.

Develop a Support System

Even though solopreneurs work independently, it's important not to isolate yourself. Building a support system of peers, mentors, and friends can provide you with the emotional and practical support you need to manage stress.

Here's how to develop a support system:

Join solopreneur or entrepreneurial communities: There are many online and local communities for solopreneurs where you can connect with others facing similar challenges. Platforms like LinkedIn, Facebook, or industry-specific forums provide opportunities to network, share advice, and gain support from fellow business owners.

Seek out mentors or coaches: A mentor or business coach can offer valuable guidance and insight based on their experience. Having someone to turn to for advice, especially during difficult times, can help you gain perspective and develop solutions to your challenges.

Collaborate with other solopreneurs: Collaboration with other solopreneurs can create a sense of camaraderie and reduce the feelings of isolation. Whether it's working on joint projects, sharing resources, or simply exchanging ideas, collaborating can help you stay motivated and feel supported.

Stay connected with friends and family: It's easy to become so focused on your business that you neglect personal relationships. Make time for friends and family to maintain emotional balance. They can provide comfort, encouragement, and a break from the stresses of work.

Having a strong support network ensures that you don't have to navigate the challenges of solopreneurship alone. Whether it's a mentor offering advice or a peer providing encouragement, your support system can help you stay resilient.

Practice Stress Management Techniques

When stress levels rise, it's important to have effective stress management techniques that allow you to release tension and regain your focus. Developing a toolkit of techniques that work for you can help you stay calm and centered, even during stressful times.

Here are some stress management techniques to practice:

Deep breathing: Deep breathing exercises can help calm your nervous system and reduce the physical symptoms of stress. Try the 4-7-8 breathing technique: inhale for four counts, hold your breath for seven counts, and exhale for eight counts. Repeat this a few times to relax.

Progressive muscle relaxation: This technique involves tensing and then relaxing different muscle groups in your body. Start by tensing your feet, holding for a few seconds, and then releasing. Move up through your body, focusing on each muscle group. This helps release physical tension and promote relaxation.

Time out for mindfulness: Take short breaks throughout your day to practice mindfulness. During these breaks, step away from work, clear your mind, and focus on being present. Mindful moments can be as simple as focusing on your breath, listening to calming music, or taking a brief walk outside.

Creative outlets: Engaging in creative activities like drawing, writing, playing an instrument, or crafting can help you relax and de-stress. Creative outlets give your mind a break from work and allow you to express yourself in a different way.

Take regular breaks: Working non-stop without breaks can lead to burnout. Schedule regular breaks throughout your workday, whether it's a short walk, stretching, or simply stepping away from your desk for a few minutes. Breaks help recharge your mind and prevent stress from building up.

By practicing stress management techniques regularly, you can build resilience and prevent stress from overwhelming you.

Set Realistic Expectations and Goals

As a solopreneur, it's easy to place high expectations on yourself to do everything perfectly or achieve success quickly. However, unrealistic expectations can increase stress and lead to frustration when things don't go as planned. Setting realistic goals and managing your expectations is crucial for reducing stress and building resilience.

Here's how to set realistic expectations:

Break goals into smaller steps: Instead of focusing on large, daunting goals, break them down into smaller, more manageable steps. This makes your goals feel more achievable and reduces the pressure to accomplish everything at once. Celebrate each step you complete, as this helps you feel progress without getting overwhelmed.

Be patient with yourself: Building a successful business takes time, and setbacks are a natural part of the journey. Be patient with yourself and recognize that progress, no matter how small, is still progress. Give yourself permission to make mistakes and learn from them.

Avoid perfectionism: Perfectionism can create unnecessary stress by making you feel like nothing is ever good enough. Aim for progress, not perfection, and understand that done is better than perfect. Allow yourself to make decisions and move forward without getting stuck in the pursuit of flawlessness.

Re-evaluate your goals regularly: As your business evolves, your goals and priorities may change. Periodically reassess your goals to ensure they still align with your vision and capabilities. Adjust your expectations based on your current circumstances, and give yourself flexibility to adapt.

By setting realistic goals and managing your expectations, you can reduce stress and avoid feeling overwhelmed by the demands of solopreneurship.

Learn to Delegate and Outsource

One of the main sources of stress for solopreneurs is the pressure to do everything themselves. While solopreneurship often requires wearing many hats, trying to handle every aspect of your business can lead to burnout. Learning to delegate or outsource tasks can help reduce stress and free up time for higher-value work.

Here's how to effectively delegate and outsource:

Identify tasks that can be outsourced: Look at your daily and weekly tasks and identify those that don't require your personal attention or expertise. Tasks like bookkeeping, administrative work, social media management, and graphic design can often be outsourced to freelancers or virtual assistants.

Hire freelancers or contractors: Hiring freelancers for specific tasks allows you to tap into their expertise without committing to a full-time employee. Websites like Upwork, Fiverr, and Freelancer provide access to a wide range of skilled professionals who can help lighten your workload.

Trust others to handle tasks: Once you've delegated or outsourced tasks, trust the person or team you've hired to get the job done. Micromanaging can create more stress and defeat the purpose of delegating. Clearly communicate your expectations and provide feedback, but give them the autonomy to complete the task.

Focus on high-value activities: By outsourcing repetitive or time-consuming tasks, you can focus your energy on activities that directly contribute to the growth of your business, such as product development, client relationships, and strategic planning.

Learning to delegate and outsource can alleviate stress and help you maintain a healthier balance between your work and personal life.

Conclusion

Solopreneurship comes with its share of stress, but by building resilience and learning how to manage that stress effectively, you can thrive in your business and avoid burnout. By recognizing your stressors, prioritizing self-care, building a support system, and practicing stress management techniques, you can navigate challenges with greater ease.

Remember that building a successful business is a marathon, not a sprint. By setting realistic goals, delegating tasks when necessary, and maintaining a positive outlook, you'll be better equipped to handle the inevitable ups and downs of solopreneurship. Resilience is not about avoiding stress entirely; it's about learning to bounce back, adapt, and keep moving forward, even in the face of adversity. With the right strategies in place, you can not only manage stress but use it as a tool for growth and personal development as a solopreneur.

The Role of Online Communities in Solopreneur Success

Online communities have become an essential resource for solopreneurs, offering a space for learning, networking, support, and collaboration. Running a business on your own can feel isolating at times, and being part of an online community provides a sense of connection and shared experience. Solopreneurs can access valuable insights from others who have faced similar challenges, exchange ideas, and get practical advice to grow their businesses.

In this chapter, we'll explore the role that online communities play in solopreneur success and how you can leverage these networks to improve your business, find support, and stay motivated.

The Value of Connection and Support

One of the main reasons solopreneurs turn to online communities is the need for connection and support. When you're running a business alone, it's easy to feel isolated, especially if you don't have a team or colleagues to brainstorm with. Online communities offer a way to connect with other solopreneurs, freelancers, and entrepreneurs who understand the unique challenges of working independently.

Here's how online communities provide valuable connection and support:

Shared experiences: Within these communities, solopreneurs can share their experiences, challenges, and successes with others who are on similar journeys. This sense of shared experience creates a supportive environment where members can give and receive encouragement.

Emotional support: Running a business can be stressful, and it's important to have a support system in place. Online communities offer a space where you can express frustrations or celebrate wins without judgment. Other members can provide emotional support, offer advice, and remind you that you're not alone.

Accountability: Many solopreneurs use online communities to find accountability partners. Whether it's working on a shared goal, setting weekly milestones, or checking in on each other's progress, accountability partners help you stay focused and motivated.

By participating in online communities, solopreneurs can reduce feelings of isolation and build relationships with others who are facing similar challenges. These connections foster a sense of belonging and can be invaluable during difficult times.

Learning and Skill Development

Online communities are a treasure trove of knowledge and resources. Solopreneurs often need to develop new skills quickly—whether it's marketing, web design, or managing finances—and these communities can provide access to expert advice, tutorials, and resources that can help you grow your business.

Here's how online communities contribute to learning and skill development:

Access to expertise: Many online communities are home to experienced entrepreneurs, industry experts, and professionals who are willing to share their knowledge. Whether you're looking for marketing tips, advice on business development, or technical support, these experts can offer guidance and practical solutions to your challenges.

Workshops and webinars: Many online communities host regular workshops, webinars, or live events focused on specific topics, such as social media marketing, time management, or product development. These events offer solopreneurs the opportunity to learn from experts in a structured format and gain valuable insights that they can apply to their businesses.

Peer-to-peer learning: Solopreneurs can learn from one another by sharing personal experiences, challenges, and solutions. Peer-to-peer learning creates a collaborative environment where members exchange ideas, recommend tools, and offer feedback. Learning from the successes and mistakes of others can help you avoid common pitfalls and improve your own business practices.

Access to resources: Online communities often share a wealth of resources, including articles, eBooks, templates, checklists, and case studies. These resources can help solopreneurs build their knowledge base and implement proven strategies in their businesses.

By actively participating in online communities, solopreneurs can stay up-to-date on industry trends, develop new skills, and gain insights that directly impact their business success.

Networking and Collaboration Opportunities

Networking is essential for business growth, and online communities provide solopreneurs with the opportunity to build meaningful relationships with other professionals. These connections can lead to collaboration, partnerships, and even new clients. Unlike traditional networking events, which may be limited by geography, online communities give you access to a global network of entrepreneurs and business owners.

Here's how online communities foster networking and collaboration:

Building relationships: Online communities offer a space for solopreneurs to interact, build rapport, and establish relationships with others in their industry or niche. These connections can lead to future collaborations, partnerships, or referrals.

Collaborative projects: Many solopreneurs collaborate with others they meet through online communities on joint projects, such as webinars, content creation, or product launches. Collaborating with others allows you to leverage each other's strengths, expand your audience, and create new opportunities for business growth.

Finding clients or partners: Online communities can be a great place to find new clients or business partners. By building relationships and demonstrating your expertise, you may attract potential clients who need your services or find collaborators who can help you expand your business offerings.

Industry networking: Some online communities are industry-specific, providing opportunities to connect with others in your field or niche. These connections can lead to valuable industry insights, partnerships, and the sharing of best practices. Networking within your industry can also help you stay informed about trends and opportunities.

By actively engaging in online communities, solopreneurs can expand their professional network, create collaboration opportunities, and build relationships that contribute to long-term success.

Access to Tools and Resources

Solopreneurs often rely on tools and software to streamline their business operations, but finding the right tools can be overwhelming. Online communities are an excellent source of recommendations for the best tools, apps, and resources to help you run your business more efficiently. Community members often share reviews, tutorials, and tips on how to make the most of different tools, saving you time and helping you avoid trial-and-error.

Here's how online communities provide access to valuable tools and resources:

Software recommendations: Whether you're looking for project management software, accounting tools, or marketing automation platforms, online communities offer real-world reviews and recommendations. Other solopreneurs can share their experiences with specific tools and help you choose the best options for your business needs.

Resource sharing: Many online communities share resources such as templates, spreadsheets, eBooks, and guides that solopreneurs can use to improve their business processes. For example, you might find a content calendar template, a financial budgeting tool, or a marketing strategy checklist that can streamline your workflow.

Tutorials and guides: In addition to recommendations, online communities often provide step-by-step tutorials and guides on how to use different tools effectively. These tutorials can help you get up to speed quickly and make the most of the resources at your disposal.

Exclusive discounts and offers: Some online communities partner with software providers or service companies to offer exclusive discounts or promotions to their members. These offers can help you access premium tools or services at a lower cost, making it easier to invest in your business.

By leveraging the tools and resources shared within online communities, solopreneurs can improve their efficiency, save time, and reduce costs.

Staying Motivated and Accountable

One of the challenges solopreneurs face is staying motivated, especially when working alone for long periods. Online communities provide an environment where solopreneurs can share their progress, set goals, and stay accountable to others. This accountability helps keep you motivated and focused, even when you encounter obstacles or feel isolated.

Here's how online communities help with motivation and accountability:

Goal-setting challenges: Many online communities run regular challenges where members set specific goals and work together to achieve them. These challenges may be focused on business growth, personal development, or skill-building, and they create a sense of camaraderie as members support each other in reaching their objectives.

Public accountability: Sharing your goals and progress with others in an online community creates a sense of accountability. When you publicly commit to a goal, you're more likely to stay on track and follow through, knowing that others are watching your progress.

Celebrating successes: Online communities provide a space to celebrate wins, both big and small. Whether you've landed a new client, launched a product, or hit a revenue milestone, sharing your successes with others can boost your motivation and reinforce your commitment to your business.

Inspiration from peers: Seeing the progress and achievements of other solopreneurs can be incredibly inspiring. Hearing how others have overcome challenges, achieved their goals, and grown their businesses can reignite your own motivation and remind you that success is possible.

By participating in goal-setting challenges, sharing progress, and celebrating achievements, solopreneurs can stay motivated and accountable, even during tough times.

Finding New Opportunities

Online communities are often hubs of opportunity, where solopreneurs can discover new business ideas, trends, or collaborations. By staying engaged and active in these communities, you can uncover potential opportunities that you may not have considered before.

Here's how online communities help you find new opportunities:

Spotting trends: Engaging with other solopreneurs and entrepreneurs in online communities can help you stay ahead of industry trends. By keeping an ear to the ground, you can identify emerging markets, technologies, or business models that may be relevant to your business.

New business ideas: Solopreneurs often share their own experiences and business ideas in online communities. These discussions can spark inspiration for new products, services, or marketing strategies that you can implement in your own business.

Job and project opportunities: Many online communities have dedicated sections where members post job openings, freelance opportunities, or collaboration requests. These opportunities can help you find new clients, projects, or partnerships that align with your business goals.

Feedback on new ventures: If you're considering launching a new product or service, online communities provide a space to seek feedback and advice before going public. This feedback can help you refine your offering, identify potential challenges, and ensure that you're meeting the needs of your target audience.

By staying engaged and open to new ideas, solopreneurs can use online communities to discover opportunities that can fuel their business growth and success.

Online communities play a pivotal role in the success of solopreneurs by providing connection, support, learning opportunities, networking, and access to valuable resources. Whether you're looking to develop new skills, find collaboration partners, or stay motivated, these communities offer a wealth of knowledge and support that can help you thrive as a solopreneur.

By actively participating in online communities, solopreneurs can build relationships, exchange ideas, and tap into a global network of like-minded professionals who are all working toward similar goals. The connections you make and the knowledge you gain from these communities can be transformative, helping you overcome challenges, seize new opportunities, and grow your business with confidence.

How to Scale Your Solopreneur Business

Scaling a solopreneur business is a crucial step for growth, but it can be a daunting process, especially when you're the only one responsible for every aspect of the business. The good news is that with strategic planning and the right systems in place, you can successfully expand your business without sacrificing quality or overburdening yourself.

In this chapter, we'll explore practical strategies for scaling your solopreneur business, from optimizing your processes to outsourcing, leveraging technology, and diversifying your income streams. Scaling doesn't necessarily mean you have to hire a team; it's about growing your business in a sustainable way that allows you to increase revenue while managing your time and resources effectively.

Optimize and Automate Your Processes

The first step in scaling your business is to optimize and streamline your existing processes. This involves identifying inefficiencies, eliminating redundant tasks, and automating repetitive processes to free up your time for higher-value activities. When your business operations are running smoothly, it becomes easier to manage increased demand.

Here's how to optimize and automate your business processes:

Identify inefficiencies: Take a close look at your day-to-day operations and pinpoint areas where you're spending too much time or where processes are slowing you down. Are you manually sending invoices? Are you spending hours responding to emails? Identifying these bottlenecks helps you figure out where improvements can be made.

Leverage automation tools: Automation can significantly reduce the amount of time you spend on administrative tasks. For example, you can use tools like QuickBooks or FreshBooks to automate invoicing and bookkeeping, Buffer or Hootsuite for scheduling social media posts, and Mailchimp or ConvertKit to automate email marketing campaigns. Automation frees you from repetitive tasks, allowing you to focus on growth-related activities.

Create workflows: Establish clear workflows for routine tasks to ensure consistency and efficiency. Whether it's how you onboard clients, handle customer support, or process orders, having a documented workflow helps streamline your operations and makes it easier to delegate in the future.

Track your time: Use time-tracking tools like Toggl or RescueTime to monitor how you're spending your time. This helps you identify tasks that could be delegated, outsourced, or automated, and ensures that you're focusing on the most important aspects of your business.

By optimizing and automating your processes, you'll be better equipped to handle increased workload as your business scales.

OUTSOURCE NON-CORE Tasks

As a solopreneur, trying to do everything yourself can limit your ability to grow. Outsourcing non-core tasks allows you to focus on the areas of your business that require your expertise and attention, while delegating time-consuming tasks to freelancers or contractors.

Here's how to approach outsourcing:

Identify tasks to outsource: Consider outsourcing tasks that don't require your direct involvement or specialized knowledge, such as administrative work, customer service, graphic design, or content creation. These tasks can be handled by virtual assistants, freelancers, or agencies.

Find reliable freelancers: Use platforms like Upwork, Fiverr, or Freelancer to find skilled professionals who can take on specific tasks or projects. When outsourcing, it's important to vet freelancers carefully by reviewing their portfolios, reading client reviews, and conducting interviews to ensure they're a good fit for your business.

Start small: If you're new to outsourcing, start with small, manageable tasks to test the waters. As you build trust with your freelancers, you can gradually delegate more responsibilities. This allows you to maintain control over your business while freeing up time to focus on growth.

Focus on core competencies: By outsourcing non-core tasks, you can dedicate more time to activities that directly impact your business growth, such as product development, marketing strategy, and client relations.

Outsourcing is a powerful way to scale your solopreneur business without the need to hire full-time employees, giving you the flexibility to grow while maintaining control over your operations.

Leverage Technology to Increase Efficiency

Technology is a key enabler for solopreneurs looking to scale their business. By leveraging the right tools and platforms, you can automate processes, manage tasks more efficiently, and improve your overall productivity.

Here's how to use technology to scale your business:

Project management tools: Tools like Asana, Trello, or Monday.com help you organize tasks, set deadlines, and track progress. These tools are especially helpful when managing multiple projects or working with freelancers, as they allow you to keep everything on track and ensure timely delivery.

CRM systems: A Customer Relationship Management (CRM) system like HubSpot, Zoho CRM, or Salesforce helps you manage leads, track customer interactions, and nurture client relationships. By automating aspects of client communication, you can ensure that no leads slip through the cracks and that customer inquiries are handled promptly.

E-commerce platforms: If you sell physical or digital products, platforms like Shopify, WooCommerce, or Etsy provide the infrastructure you need to scale your sales. These platforms offer tools for managing inventory, processing payments, and fulfilling orders, making it easier to handle an increased volume of sales.

Analytics tools: Google Analytics, SEMrush, or Ahrefs provide valuable insights into your website traffic, customer behavior, and marketing performance. By analyzing this data, you can make informed decisions about where to focus your marketing efforts and how to optimize your website or campaigns for better results.

By incorporating these tools into your business, you can work more efficiently and manage the complexities of scaling with greater ease.

Diversify Your Income Streams

One of the most effective ways to scale your solopreneur business is by diversifying your income streams. Relying on a single product or service can limit your growth potential, while offering multiple products or services creates new opportunities for revenue generation and reduces risk.

Here's how to diversify your income:

Offer new services: If you're a service-based solopreneur, consider offering additional services that complement your existing offerings. For example, a freelance writer might offer editing services, or a marketing consultant might provide social media management. Expanding your service portfolio allows you to serve a wider range of clients.

Create digital products: Digital products, such as eBooks, online courses, or templates, are a great way to generate passive income. Once created, these products can be sold repeatedly without requiring additional time or effort on your part. This allows you to scale your revenue without increasing your workload.

Monetize content: If you have a blog, YouTube channel, or podcast, consider monetizing your content through advertising, sponsorships, or affiliate marketing. These income streams can supplement your primary business while allowing you to reach new audiences and build your brand.

Develop a subscription model: A subscription-based business model, such as offering a membership site or exclusive content, provides recurring revenue and helps build long-term relationships with customers. This model can be applied to various industries, from coaching to digital products, and creates a more predictable income stream.

Diversifying your income streams not only increases your earning potential but also makes your business more resilient in the face of market changes or fluctuations in demand.

BUILD SCALABLE MARKETING Strategies

To scale your business, you need to attract more customers, and that means scaling your marketing efforts. However, as a solopreneur, it's important to focus on marketing strategies that are scalable, meaning they can be replicated and expanded without requiring a proportional increase in time or resources.

Here's how to build scalable marketing strategies:

Content marketing: Creating high-quality content, such as blog posts, videos, or podcasts, helps you attract organic traffic and build brand authority over time. Once published, content continues to work for you by driving traffic, generating leads, and improving SEO, all without requiring ongoing effort. Focus on creating evergreen content that remains relevant and valuable to your audience over the long term.

Email marketing: Building an email list allows you to nurture relationships with potential customers and keep your audience engaged. Email marketing can be automated through tools like Mailchimp or ActiveCampaign, allowing you to send targeted messages, promotions, or newsletters at scale.

Paid advertising: Platforms like Google Ads, Facebook Ads, or Instagram Ads offer highly targeted advertising options that allow you to reach a larger audience without significant time investment. Paid ads can be scaled up based on your budget and marketing goals, making them an effective way to drive traffic and conversions as your business grows.

SEO optimization: Search engine optimization (SEO) ensures that your website ranks higher in search engine results, driving organic traffic over time. By investing in SEO strategies, such as optimizing your website content, building backlinks, and targeting relevant keywords, you can attract more visitors without ongoing effort.

By focusing on scalable marketing strategies, you can increase your brand's visibility and attract more customers without overextending yourself.

Build Systems for Growth

As your business scales, building systems that support long-term growth is essential. Systems help you manage increased demand, maintain quality, and ensure consistency, even as your business expands.

Here's how to build systems for growth:

Standardize your processes: Create standard operating procedures (SOPs) for recurring tasks to ensure that they are completed consistently and efficiently. SOPs are especially useful if you plan to delegate tasks or bring on freelancers, as they provide clear instructions on how things should be done.

Focus on customer retention: As your business grows, it's important to build systems for retaining customers and nurturing relationships. Implement strategies for maintaining customer loyalty, such as offering personalized experiences, sending follow-up emails, or creating a loyalty program.

Invest in scalability: When choosing tools, platforms, or services, ensure they can scale with your business. For example, if you're using e-commerce software, select one that can handle increased traffic and sales volume as your business grows. Planning for scalability from the outset reduces the need for major changes later on.

Track key performance indicators (KPIs): Monitoring KPIs allows you to measure the success of your growth efforts and make data-driven decisions. Whether it's tracking website traffic, conversion rates, or customer acquisition costs, regularly reviewing your KPIs helps you identify areas for improvement and optimize your business for growth.

By building systems that support scalability, you'll be able to manage growth more effectively and ensure that your business can continue to thrive as it expands.

Scaling a solopreneur business is both an exciting and challenging process. While it requires careful planning and strategic decision-making, the rewards can be substantial. By optimizing your processes, leveraging technology, outsourcing non-core tasks, and diversifying your income streams, you can successfully grow your business without burning out.

Building scalable marketing strategies, focusing on customer retention, and creating systems for growth are all key elements of scaling sustainably. As you implement these strategies, you'll be better positioned to handle increased demand, improve efficiency, and achieve long-term success as a solopreneur. Remember, scaling isn't about doing more—it's about doing things smarter, so you can grow your business while maintaining control over your time and resources.

Online Resources Every Solopreneur Should Know

In today's digital world, solopreneurs have access to a vast array of online resources that can help them streamline operations, market their businesses, improve skills, and scale more effectively. Whether you're looking for tools to automate tasks, platforms to find freelancers, or educational content to enhance your knowledge, the right resources can make a significant difference in your productivity and success as a solopreneur.

In this chapter, we'll explore essential online resources that every solopreneur should know about. These tools, platforms, and websites can help you manage your business more efficiently, connect with others, and access the support you need to thrive.

Project Management Tools

Staying organized is key to managing multiple tasks and projects effectively, especially when you're the only one handling everything. Project management tools help solopreneurs plan, prioritize, and track progress on tasks while maintaining clarity on deadlines and deliverables.

Here are some popular project management tools:

Trello: Trello uses a simple card-and-board system that helps you organize tasks, projects, and workflows visually. It's user-friendly and great for solopreneurs who prefer a more flexible and visual approach to project management.

Asana: Asana allows you to organize tasks, assign deadlines, and track progress with ease. It's perfect for solopreneurs managing multiple projects or collaborating with freelancers.

Monday.com: A highly customizable project management platform, Monday.com helps solopreneurs plan, execute, and track projects in one place. It offers automation features that can save time on repetitive tasks.

ClickUp: ClickUp is an all-in-one platform that combines task management, goal setting, time tracking, and document sharing. It's highly flexible and can be tailored to fit the needs of solopreneurs in various industries.

These project management tools help solopreneurs stay organized, manage workflows, and ensure nothing slips through the cracks.

Accounting and Invoicing Software

Managing finances is one of the most important aspects of running a successful solopreneur business. Accounting and invoicing software can simplify financial tasks such as tracking income and expenses, sending invoices, managing taxes, and generating reports.

Here are some of the best accounting and invoicing tools:

QuickBooks: QuickBooks is a comprehensive accounting solution that handles everything from invoicing and expense tracking to payroll and tax preparation. It's ideal for solopreneurs who need a robust platform to manage their finances.

FreshBooks: Known for its simplicity and ease of use, FreshBooks is great for solopreneurs who want a straightforward invoicing and expense management system. It offers features such as time tracking, project management, and automated payment reminders.

Wave: Wave is a free accounting and invoicing tool that offers many features similar to paid software. It's perfect for solopreneurs on a budget who still need to manage invoices, track expenses, and generate financial reports.

Xero: Xero provides a comprehensive suite of accounting tools that include invoicing, payroll, inventory management, and financial reporting. It's a scalable solution for solopreneurs looking to grow their business.

Using accounting software allows solopreneurs to manage their finances more efficiently, reducing the risk of errors and saving time on manual bookkeeping tasks.

Marketing Automation Tools

Marketing automation is essential for solopreneurs who want to scale their marketing efforts without dedicating countless hours to manual tasks. These tools allow you to automate emails, social media posts, and other marketing activities so you can reach a larger audience while focusing on other areas of your business.

Here are some of the best marketing automation tools for solopreneurs:

Mailchimp: Mailchimp is a popular email marketing platform that offers automation features such as drip campaigns, A/B testing, and analytics. It's great for solopreneurs looking to build and nurture their email list.

ConvertKit: ConvertKit is an email marketing tool designed for creators, such as bloggers, coaches, and small business owners. It offers automation features that allow you to create email sequences based on subscriber behavior.

Buffer: Buffer is a social media scheduling tool that allows you to plan and automate posts across platforms like Facebook, Instagram, and Twitter. It's perfect for solopreneurs who want to maintain a consistent social media presence without having to post in real time.

Hootsuite: Hootsuite is another social media management platform that allows you to schedule posts, track social media engagement, and analyze the performance of your campaigns. It's great for solopreneurs managing multiple social media accounts.

HubSpot: HubSpot offers a range of marketing automation tools, including email marketing, lead nurturing, and CRM integration. While it has a free version, HubSpot is ideal for solopreneurs looking to scale their marketing efforts and manage customer relationships.

These marketing automation tools can help solopreneurs save time, reach more people, and nurture leads more effectively.

Content Creation Tools

Creating high-quality content is essential for solopreneurs looking to attract customers, build their brand, and engage with their audience. Whether it's blog posts, videos, or social media graphics, content creation tools make the process easier and more professional.

Here are some top content creation tools for solopreneurs:

Canva: Canva is a user-friendly graphic design tool that allows solopreneurs to create stunning visuals for social media, websites, blogs, and marketing materials. It offers thousands of templates and design elements, making it easy to create professional-looking graphics, even without design experience.

Lumen5: Lumen5 is a video creation platform that turns blog posts or written content into engaging videos. It's perfect for solopreneurs who want to create video content quickly without having to film or edit video footage themselves.

Grammarly: Grammarly is a writing assistant that helps solopreneurs improve their writing by checking for grammar, punctuation, tone, and style issues. It's a must-have tool for anyone producing written content, whether it's blog posts, emails, or social media captions.

Unsplash: Unsplash offers high-quality, royalty-free stock images that solopreneurs can use for blogs, social media, and marketing materials. It's a valuable resource for finding visually appealing images without paying for stock photo subscriptions.

Giphy: If you want to add some fun and engagement to your social media posts or emails, Giphy provides a huge collection of GIFs that you can use to communicate visually and entertain your audience.

By leveraging these content creation tools, solopreneurs can produce engaging, high-quality content that elevates their brand and helps attract more customers.

Freelance and Outsourcing Platforms

Solopreneurs often need to outsource specific tasks to freelancers or contractors. Whether it's web development, graphic design, writing, or virtual assistance, freelance platforms make it easy to find skilled professionals who can help with one-off projects or ongoing support.

Here are some popular freelance and outsourcing platforms:

Upwork: Upwork is one of the largest freelance platforms, offering access to a wide range of professionals across industries. Solopreneurs can post job listings and hire freelancers for tasks such as writing, design, marketing, and development.

Fiverr: Fiverr is ideal for solopreneurs looking for affordable freelance services. Freelancers on Fiverr offer services starting at $5, making it an attractive option for those with smaller budgets. You can find services ranging from logo design to video editing.

Freelancer: Similar to Upwork, Freelancer connects solopreneurs with skilled freelancers in various fields. The platform allows you to post projects, review bids, and select freelancers based on their portfolios and ratings.

99designs: 99designs specializes in graphic design services, making it the go-to platform for solopreneurs in need of logos, branding materials, or web design. It works as a design contest where multiple designers submit work, and you choose the one you like best.

Toptal: If you need highly specialized freelancers, Toptal provides access to the top 3% of freelance talent, including developers, designers, and finance experts. It's a premium option for solopreneurs seeking top-tier professionals.

Outsourcing tasks to freelancers allows solopreneurs to focus on core business activities while tapping into specialized skills for areas they may not have expertise in.

Learning and Development Platforms

Continuous learning is essential for solopreneurs who want to stay ahead of industry trends and improve their skills. Online learning platforms provide access to courses, tutorials, and resources on everything from marketing to finance, technology, and personal development.

Here are some valuable learning and development platforms:

Udemy: Udemy offers thousands of online courses on a wide range of topics, from digital marketing and web development to personal development and leadership. It's a great resource for solopreneurs looking to expand their knowledge or gain new skills.

Coursera: Coursera partners with top universities and institutions to offer high-quality online courses and certifications. Solopreneurs can access courses on business, technology, and creative fields to further their education and build expertise.

Skillshare: Skillshare is a subscription-based platform that offers creative courses on design, photography, writing, and entrepreneurship. It's perfect for solopreneurs looking to develop creative skills and explore new business ideas.

LinkedIn Learning: LinkedIn Learning provides professional development courses on business, technology, and creative skills. It's a valuable platform for solopreneurs who want to learn practical skills that can be directly applied to their businesses.

YouTube: While often overlooked as an educational resource, YouTube offers thousands of free tutorials and instructional videos on virtually every topic imaginable. Solopreneurs can find valuable content on everything from business strategy to marketing techniques.

By leveraging these learning platforms, solopreneurs can stay up to date with the latest trends, improve their skills, and continue growing both personally and professionally.

Conclusion

The right online resources can make a world of difference for solopreneurs, allowing them to manage their businesses more efficiently, create high-quality content, outsource tasks, and continue learning and growing. From project management and marketing automation tools to freelance platforms and educational resources, these tools can help you streamline operations, increase productivity, and scale your business effectively.

By integrating these essential online resources into your business strategy, you'll be better equipped to handle the challenges of solopreneurship and set yourself up for long-term success. Whether you're just starting out or looking to grow, these tools and platforms can support you at every stage of your solopreneur journey.

Embracing Failure as Part of the Solopreneur Journey

Failure is often viewed as something to be avoided, but in the world of solopreneurship, failure can be one of the most valuable learning experiences. It's an inevitable part of the journey, and every setback, mistake, or failure holds the potential to teach you something crucial for your future success. Embracing failure not only helps you build resilience but also gives you the tools to adapt, grow, and refine your approach to business.

In this chapter, we'll explore how solopreneurs can embrace failure as a natural part of their journey and use it as a stepping stone to greater success. By shifting your perspective on failure, you'll be able to navigate challenges with confidence and turn obstacles into opportunities for growth.

Shifting Your Mindset on Failure

The first step in embracing failure is shifting your mindset. Many solopreneurs view failure as a reflection of their abilities or as a sign that they aren't cut out for the entrepreneurial journey. However, failure is often a natural part of taking risks, learning new things, and growing as a business owner. Instead of fearing failure, see it as a learning experience that moves you closer to success.

Here's how to shift your mindset on failure:

View failure as feedback: Failure isn't a dead end—it's feedback. Every time something doesn't go as planned, you gain valuable insights into what went wrong and why. Instead of seeing failure as an end point, view it as data that can guide your future decisions. Ask yourself: What did I learn from this? How can I improve my approach next time?

Detach from perfectionism: Solopreneurs often feel immense pressure to get everything right the first time. However, striving for perfection can lead to paralysis and prevent you from taking risks. Recognize that perfection is unattainable, and that mistakes and missteps are part of the process. Embrace imperfection as a sign of progress and growth.

Celebrate risk-taking: Every time you take a calculated risk, you're moving out of your comfort zone and pushing the boundaries of what's possible. Even if that risk doesn't pay off immediately, celebrate the fact that you had the courage to take it. Over time, these risks will yield valuable results.

By changing the way you think about failure, you'll be better equipped to handle setbacks and keep moving forward with a growth mindset.

Learning from Failure

Every failure holds lessons that can help you improve your business strategy, refine your skills, and make better decisions. The key to learning from failure is reflecting on your experiences, identifying the root causes of the failure, and making adjustments to avoid similar mistakes in the future.

Here's how to learn from failure:

Analyze what went wrong: After experiencing a failure, take the time to analyze what went wrong. Was it a lack of planning, poor execution, or misjudging market demand? Understanding the specific reasons for the failure helps you pinpoint areas that need improvement. Be honest with yourself, but avoid being overly critical. The goal is to learn, not to dwell on the past.

Identify patterns: If you experience repeated failures in the same area, such as marketing campaigns that don't convert or products that don't sell, look for patterns. Identifying recurring mistakes can help you address underlying issues that may be holding you back.

Ask for feedback: Sometimes, the best way to learn from failure is to seek outside perspectives. Ask trusted peers, mentors, or even customers for feedback on what might have gone wrong. They may offer insights you hadn't considered and provide a more objective view of the situation.

Apply your lessons: The most important part of learning from failure is applying what you've learned. Whether it's adjusting your pricing strategy, improving your customer service, or refining your marketing tactics, take action based on the insights you gained from your failure. Over time, these adjustments will lead to better outcomes.

By treating failure as a learning opportunity, you can continuously improve and refine your business strategies, setting yourself up for future success.

Building Resilience through Failure

Failure can be tough, especially when you've poured your heart and soul into your business. However, each failure also presents an opportunity to build resilience. Resilience is the ability to bounce back from setbacks, adapt to change, and keep pushing forward in the face of adversity. It's a critical trait for solopreneurs, as the path to success is rarely a straight line.

Here's how to build resilience through failure:

Reframe setbacks as temporary: When faced with failure, it's easy to fall into the trap of thinking that the setback is permanent. However, most failures are temporary roadblocks, not permanent dead ends. Reframing setbacks as temporary challenges helps you stay focused on finding solutions and moving forward.

Practice self-compassion: Solopreneurs can be their own harshest critics, especially when things don't go as planned. Practicing self-compassion means treating yourself with kindness and understanding, rather than being overly critical. Remind yourself that failure is a normal part of the entrepreneurial journey and that setbacks don't define your worth or abilities.

Focus on long-term vision: Resilience comes from staying connected to your long-term vision, even when short-term setbacks occur. When you face failure, remind yourself of your bigger goals and why you started your business in the first place. This sense of purpose will keep you motivated and focused on the bigger picture.

Develop a "failure recovery" routine: Having a routine to help you recover from failure can make a significant difference in how quickly you bounce back. This might include taking a break to clear your mind, talking to a mentor for support, or engaging in a physical activity that helps reduce stress. Building healthy coping mechanisms helps you manage the emotional toll of failure and move forward more quickly.

Resilience is built over time, and each failure you overcome strengthens your ability to handle future challenges with confidence and grace.

Using Failure as a Tool for Innovation

Some of the most successful businesses were born out of failure. When things don't go as planned, it often forces solopreneurs to think creatively and come up with innovative solutions. Failure can be a catalyst for innovation, pushing you to explore new ideas, pivot your strategy, or create something entirely different.

Here's how to use failure as a tool for innovation:

Look for hidden opportunities: Failure can reveal opportunities that you may not have considered before. For example, if a product launch doesn't go as planned, you might discover a different audience or market niche that's better suited to your offering. Stay curious and open to new possibilities that arise from failure.

Experiment and iterate: Innovation often comes from experimentation. When something fails, treat it as a chance to experiment with new approaches. Test different strategies, tweak your offerings, and iterate on your ideas until you find what works. Failure gives you the freedom to experiment without the pressure of perfection.

Embrace flexibility: Solopreneurs who succeed in the long run are often those who remain flexible and willing to pivot when necessary. Failure can be a sign that it's time to change direction, whether that means refining your business model, offering a new product, or entering a different market. Being flexible allows you to adapt to changing circumstances and stay ahead of the curve.

Foster a culture of innovation: Even as a solopreneur, you can foster a mindset of innovation within your business. Encourage yourself to take risks, try new things, and embrace failure as part of the creative process. Innovation thrives when you give yourself permission to fail and learn from those failures.

By using failure as a tool for innovation, you'll be able to discover new opportunities and stay agile in a constantly changing business environment.

Sharing Your Failures with Others

One of the most powerful ways to embrace failure is by sharing your experiences with others. Solopreneurs often feel pressure to present an image of constant success, but being open about your failures can build trust, inspire others, and foster a sense of community. Sharing your failures not only helps you process them, but it also allows others to learn from your experiences.

Here's how sharing your failures can benefit both you and others:

Build authenticity: Being transparent about your failures humanizes your brand and builds authenticity. Customers and peers appreciate honesty, and sharing your struggles makes you more relatable. It shows that you're willing to take risks and learn from your mistakes, which can foster deeper connections with your audience.

Inspire others: Your story of overcoming failure can be a source of inspiration for others who are going through similar challenges. By sharing how you navigated setbacks and came out stronger, you can encourage fellow solopreneurs to keep going, even when things get tough.

Create a supportive community: Sharing your failures can open the door to deeper connections with others in your industry. When solopreneurs are open about their struggles, it creates a culture of support and collaboration. Others may offer advice, share their own experiences, or provide encouragement, helping you move forward with renewed confidence.

Learn from others: When you share your failures, others may share theirs in return. This exchange of experiences can be incredibly valuable, as it allows you to learn from a wider range of mistakes and solutions. By engaging in open dialogue about failure, you can gain insights that help you grow both personally and professionally.

Sharing your failures can be a powerful way to connect with others, build resilience, and inspire those around you to embrace failure as part of their own solopreneur journey.

Failure is an unavoidable part of the solopreneur journey, but it doesn't have to be feared or avoided. By embracing failure as a natural and valuable part of the process, you can learn from your mistakes, build resilience, and use setbacks as a catalyst for innovation and growth. Shifting your mindset, learning from your experiences, and staying flexible will help you navigate the challenges of solopreneurship with confidence and grace.

Remember, every failure is a stepping stone toward success. It's not about avoiding failure, but about how you respond to it and what you learn along the way. By embracing failure, you'll develop the strength, creativity, and insight needed to achieve your long-term goals and thrive as a solopreneur.

How to Stay Motivated When You're Working Alone

Staying motivated as a solopreneur can be challenging, especially when you're working alone. Without a team or colleagues to offer support or hold you accountable, maintaining focus and energy on your tasks can sometimes feel like an uphill battle. However, with the right strategies and mindset, it's possible to stay motivated and productive, even when working solo.

In this chapter, we'll explore practical ways to stay motivated when you're working alone. From setting clear goals to creating a structured routine, finding ways to connect with others, and celebrating small wins, these strategies will help you maintain momentum and avoid burnout as a solopreneur.

Set Clear and Achievable Goals

One of the most effective ways to stay motivated is by setting clear and achievable goals. When you have a clear direction, it's easier to stay focused and motivated, knowing exactly what you're working toward. Break down larger, long-term goals into smaller, actionable steps that you can work on day by day.

Here's how to set clear and achievable goals:

Define your big-picture vision: Start by defining your overarching business goals or vision. Whether it's increasing revenue, launching a new product, or growing your customer base, having a clear long-term vision gives you a sense of purpose and direction.

Break it down into smaller tasks: Once you have your big-picture goals, break them down into smaller, actionable steps. For example, if your goal is to launch a new product, break it down into tasks like product development, marketing strategy, and customer outreach. These smaller steps make big goals feel more manageable.

Set deadlines: Deadlines create urgency and help you stay on track. Assign realistic deadlines to each task and hold yourself accountable for meeting them. The sense of accomplishment you feel when you complete a task on time will help keep you motivated.

Review and adjust regularly: Regularly review your goals and progress to ensure you're on track. If needed, adjust your goals based on new information or changing circumstances. This flexibility allows you to stay focused without feeling overwhelmed.

By setting clear and achievable goals, you create a roadmap for success, making it easier to stay motivated and focused on what matters most.

CREATE A STRUCTURED Routine

When you're working alone, it can be tempting to let your schedule slip or procrastinate on tasks. Establishing a structured routine helps create a sense of order and consistency, which can boost your productivity and keep you motivated.

Here's how to create a structured routine:

Set regular working hours: Even if you have the flexibility to work whenever you want, setting regular working hours helps you create a sense of discipline and focus. Having a consistent start and end time for your workday helps you stay on track and ensures that you're dedicating enough time to your business.

Plan your day the night before: Take a few minutes at the end of each day to plan your tasks for the following day. This helps you hit the ground running in the morning and eliminates the need to decide what to work on. Having a plan in place allows you to start the day with focus and purpose.

Prioritize important tasks: Identify your most important tasks (MITs) for each day and tackle them first. By focusing on high-priority tasks, you can make meaningful progress, which will keep you motivated throughout the day.

Incorporate breaks: Breaks are essential for maintaining energy and focus. Use techniques like the Pomodoro method, where you work in focused 25-minute intervals followed by a 5-minute break. This helps prevent burnout and keeps you mentally refreshed.

End your day with a ritual: Create a ritual to mark the end of your workday, such as reviewing your progress, clearing your workspace, or writing down what you need to focus on tomorrow. This helps you mentally transition from work mode to personal time.

A structured routine provides the consistency and discipline needed to stay motivated, even when you're working on your own.

Connect with a Support Network

Working alone doesn't mean you have to feel isolated. Building a support network of fellow solopreneurs, mentors, or business communities can help you stay motivated, inspired, and connected. Surrounding yourself with like-minded individuals who understand your journey can make a big difference in maintaining your motivation.

Here's how to connect with a support network:

Join online communities: There are many online communities and forums for solopreneurs and entrepreneurs where you can share experiences, ask for advice, and offer support to others. Platforms like LinkedIn, Facebook groups, and Reddit have active communities that focus on business growth, productivity, and solopreneurship.

Attend networking events: In-person or virtual networking events, workshops, and meetups offer valuable opportunities to connect with other solopreneurs and entrepreneurs. These events can provide fresh perspectives, spark new ideas, and help you build relationships with others in your industry.

Find an accountability partner: Pair up with another solopreneur or entrepreneur to act as accountability partners. You can check in with each other regularly to discuss progress, share challenges, and set goals. Having someone to hold you accountable can help you stay motivated and on track.

Work from co-working spaces: If working from home feels isolating, consider spending a few days a week at a co-working space. These shared workspaces provide a community of professionals and offer opportunities for networking, collaboration, and social interaction.

Connecting with a support network helps you feel less alone and provides the encouragement and inspiration needed to stay motivated.

Celebrate Small Wins

Celebrating your progress, no matter how small, is a powerful motivator. Solopreneurs often focus on big milestones and overlook the small steps that lead to success. Taking the time to acknowledge and celebrate your small wins can boost your confidence and keep you motivated to keep going.

Here's how to celebrate small wins:

Track your progress: Keep a record of your accomplishments, whether it's completing a project, gaining a new client, or hitting a revenue goal. Tracking your progress helps you see how far you've come and reinforces the fact that you're making meaningful strides.

Reward yourself: Rewarding yourself for achieving small goals creates positive reinforcement. The reward doesn't have to be extravagant—it could be taking a break, treating yourself to a favorite snack, or indulging in a relaxing activity. These small rewards help you stay motivated and enjoy the process.

Reflect on your achievements: Take time to reflect on what you've accomplished at the end of each week or month. Write down the tasks you've completed and the challenges you've overcome. Reflecting on your progress can give you a sense of pride and motivate you to keep pushing forward.

Share your wins: Sharing your successes with your support network, friends, or family can make the celebration even more meaningful. Whether it's a big achievement or a small victory, letting others know about your progress can give you the encouragement you need to keep going.

Celebrating small wins keeps you motivated by reminding you that every step forward counts, even if it's not always immediately noticeable.

STAY INSPIRED WITH Continuous Learning

As a solopreneur, staying inspired and engaged is key to maintaining motivation. One of the best ways to stay inspired is through continuous learning. Expanding your knowledge and skills not only keeps your mind engaged but also opens up new opportunities for growth and innovation.

Here's how to stay inspired through continuous learning:

Take online courses: Platforms like Udemy, Coursera, and Skillshare offer a wide range of courses on business, marketing, creativity, and personal development. Taking a course on a topic you're passionate about can reignite your enthusiasm and give you new ideas for your business.

Read books and articles: Reading books or articles related to entrepreneurship, productivity, or your industry can provide fresh insights and inspiration. Set aside time each week to read, whether it's a business book, an inspirational biography, or articles on the latest trends in your field.

Listen to podcasts: Podcasts are a great way to stay motivated while learning from others' experiences. Whether you're looking for business advice, personal development tips, or stories of successful entrepreneurs, podcasts can keep you inspired and motivated on the go.

Attend workshops or webinars: Many organizations offer free or low-cost webinars and workshops on various topics, from marketing strategies to productivity hacks. Participating in these events allows you to learn from experts and stay up-to-date with industry trends.

Staying curious and continuing to learn keeps your mind engaged and motivated, while also giving you the tools to innovate and grow your business.

Focus on Your "Why"

When motivation wanes, reconnecting with your "why" can provide the inspiration you need to keep going. Your "why" is the reason you started your business in the first place—whether it's the desire for freedom, passion for your work, or the goal of making a difference in your industry or community.

Here's how to reconnect with your "why":

Remind yourself of your mission: Write down the reasons you became a solopreneur and what you hope to achieve through your business. Keep this mission statement somewhere visible, such as on your desk or in your planner, so you can refer to it when you're feeling unmotivated.

Visualize your long-term goals: Take a few moments each day to visualize what success looks like for you. Picture yourself achieving your goals, whether it's financial freedom, building a thriving business, or making a positive impact on others. Visualization can help you stay connected to your long-term vision and reignite your motivation.

Reflect on your accomplishments: Reflect on how far you've come since you started your business. Reminding yourself of the progress you've made and the challenges you've overcome helps reinforce your commitment to your journey.

Stay aligned with your values: Ensure that the work you're doing aligns with your values and passions. When your work feels meaningful and purpose-driven, it's easier to stay motivated and engaged, even during difficult times.

Focusing on your "why" provides a sense of purpose and motivation, helping you push through challenges and stay committed to your solopreneur journey.

Staying motivated when you're working alone as a solopreneur can be challenging, but with the right strategies in place, you can maintain focus, energy, and momentum. By setting clear goals, creating a structured routine, connecting with a support network, celebrating small wins, and staying inspired through continuous learning, you can keep your motivation high even during challenging times.

Remember, motivation isn't a constant—it ebbs and flows. The key is to develop habits and practices that help you stay on track, even when motivation is low. By reconnecting with your "why" and focusing on your long-term vision, you'll be able to stay motivated and continue building a successful solopreneur business, one step at a time.

The Future of Solopreneurship: Trends to Watch

The world of solopreneurship is evolving rapidly, driven by advancements in technology, changes in consumer behavior, and shifts in the global economy. As more individuals embrace the freedom and flexibility of working for themselves, solopreneurs need to stay ahead of emerging trends that will shape the future of their businesses. Understanding these trends can help solopreneurs adapt, innovate, and thrive in an increasingly competitive market.

In this chapter, we'll explore key trends to watch in the future of solopreneurship, from the rise of automation and artificial intelligence to the growing importance of personal branding, the gig economy, and remote work. By staying informed about these trends, solopreneurs can position themselves for long-term success.

The Rise of Automation and AI

Automation and artificial intelligence (AI) are transforming the way solopreneurs operate, allowing them to streamline tasks, improve efficiency, and scale their businesses without the need for additional staff. Automation tools can handle everything from marketing and customer service to invoicing and project management, freeing up time for solopreneurs to focus on strategy and growth.

Here's how automation and AI are shaping the future of solopreneurship:

Automating repetitive tasks: Tools like Zapier, IFTTT, and HubSpot allow solopreneurs to automate routine tasks such as sending emails, managing social media posts, and tracking customer interactions. AI-powered chatbots can handle customer inquiries, freeing up time for solopreneurs to focus on higher-value activities.

AI-driven insights: AI tools like Google Analytics and SEMrush provide solopreneurs with valuable data-driven insights into customer behavior, market trends, and campaign performance. These insights help solopreneurs make informed decisions and optimize their strategies for better results.

Personalized customer experiences: AI enables solopreneurs to create personalized marketing campaigns based on customer data and behavior. From personalized email sequences to targeted product recommendations, AI can enhance the customer experience and increase engagement.

By embracing automation and AI, solopreneurs can improve efficiency, reduce costs, and scale their businesses more effectively in the coming years.

The Growth of the Gig Economy

The gig economy continues to expand, with more people opting for freelance work, contract jobs, and side hustles. For solopreneurs, this presents both opportunities and challenges. The rise of the gig economy means increased competition, but it also offers new opportunities to collaborate, outsource, and tap into a global talent pool.

Here's how the gig economy is influencing solopreneurship:

Access to global talent: Solopreneurs can easily find freelancers or contractors to handle tasks such as design, marketing, writing, and technical support. Platforms like Upwork, Fiverr, and Toptal provide access to a wide range of professionals who can help solopreneurs grow their businesses without the need to hire full-time employees.

Increased competition: As more people enter the gig economy, competition for clients and projects becomes more intense. Solopreneurs will need to differentiate themselves by offering specialized skills, high-quality service, and unique value propositions to stand out in a crowded market.

Opportunities for collaboration: The gig economy fosters collaboration among solopreneurs and freelancers, enabling them to work together on larger projects or tap into each other's expertise. By building a network of freelancers and collaborators, solopreneurs can take on bigger projects and expand their offerings.

The gig economy offers solopreneurs greater flexibility and opportunities to scale, but it also requires them to stay competitive and continually evolve their skills.

The Importance of Personal Branding

In a world where consumers have countless options, personal branding has become a critical factor in building a successful solopreneur business. A strong personal brand helps solopreneurs establish credibility, build trust with their audience, and differentiate themselves from competitors. As the marketplace becomes more saturated, personal branding will play an even more significant role in the future.

Here's why personal branding is essential for solopreneurs:

Building trust and authority: A well-crafted personal brand showcases your expertise, values, and personality, helping potential clients or customers feel connected to you. By consistently sharing valuable content and engaging with your audience, you position yourself as an authority in your field.

Differentiating from competitors: In a crowded market, your personal brand is what sets you apart from others offering similar products or services. Solopreneurs who invest in building a unique brand voice and identity are more likely to stand out and attract loyal customers.

Expanding your reach: A strong personal brand can open up opportunities beyond your core business, such as speaking engagements, partnerships, or media appearances. These opportunities can further enhance your visibility and credibility, driving more traffic to your business.

As personal branding becomes increasingly important, solopreneurs will need to invest time in developing a clear, authentic brand that resonates with their target audience.

The Rise of Remote Work and Digital Nomadism

Remote work is no longer just a trend; it's becoming the norm for many solopreneurs and businesses. The COVID-19 pandemic accelerated the shift toward remote work, and as a result, more solopreneurs are embracing the freedom of working from anywhere. Digital nomadism—where individuals travel and work remotely—has also gained popularity, offering solopreneurs the flexibility to explore new places while running their businesses.

Here's how remote work is shaping the future of solopreneurship:

Increased flexibility: The ability to work from anywhere allows solopreneurs to design a lifestyle that suits them. Whether it's working from a home office, a coworking space, or while traveling, solopreneurs can create a work environment that fosters creativity and productivity.

Access to global clients: Remote work allows solopreneurs to reach clients and customers worldwide, regardless of location. With tools like Zoom, Slack, and Google Workspace, solopreneurs can collaborate with international clients, expanding their market reach and potential income.

Work-life balance challenges: While remote work offers flexibility, it can also blur the lines between work and personal life. Solopreneurs will need to develop strong time management skills and set boundaries to maintain a healthy work-life balance.

As remote work continues to grow, solopreneurs who embrace digital tools and flexible work environments will be well-positioned for success in the future.

Sustainable and Purpose-Driven Businesses

Consumers are increasingly looking for businesses that align with their values, particularly when it comes to sustainability, social responsibility, and ethical practices. Solopreneurs who focus on building purpose-driven businesses that prioritize people and the planet are likely to thrive in the years to come.

Here's why sustainability and purpose are key trends to watch:

Consumer demand for ethical businesses: Customers are more conscious of the environmental and social impact of their purchases. Solopreneurs who incorporate sustainability into their business practices—such as using eco-friendly materials, reducing waste, or supporting social causes—can attract a loyal customer base.

Building a mission-driven brand: A purpose-driven business goes beyond profit and focuses on making a positive impact in the world. Solopreneurs with a strong mission or social cause can build deeper connections with their audience, fostering loyalty and trust.

Opportunities for innovation: The demand for sustainable solutions creates opportunities for solopreneurs to innovate in areas like green technology, ethical products, and socially responsible services. Those who can develop creative, eco-friendly solutions will be well-positioned to meet evolving consumer needs.

By focusing on sustainability and purpose, solopreneurs can build businesses that not only succeed financially but also make a positive impact on the world.

The Integration of E-commerce and Digital Products

The rise of e-commerce has made it easier than ever for solopreneurs to sell physical and digital products online. From online courses and eBooks to digital art and software, solopreneurs can create scalable, low-cost products that generate passive income. E-commerce platforms like Shopify, Etsy, and Gumroad provide the infrastructure needed to sell digital products worldwide.

Here's how e-commerce and digital products are shaping the future:

Scalability: Digital products, such as online courses or templates, can be sold repeatedly without the need for additional resources. This makes them a highly scalable income stream for solopreneurs, allowing them to generate revenue without trading time for money.

Global reach: E-commerce platforms allow solopreneurs to reach a global audience with ease. By selling products online, solopreneurs can expand their customer base beyond their local market and tap into international demand.

Lower barriers to entry: Creating and selling digital products has a low barrier to entry, making it an attractive option for solopreneurs looking to diversify their income. With minimal upfront costs, solopreneurs can test new product ideas, validate demand, and iterate quickly.

As e-commerce continues to grow, solopreneurs who embrace digital products and scalable online sales strategies will have a significant advantage in the marketplace.

The Importance of Continuous Learning and Adaptation

In an ever-changing business landscape, solopreneurs must prioritize continuous learning and adaptability to stay competitive. As new technologies emerge and consumer preferences evolve, those who invest in their own education and skills development will be better positioned to innovate and seize new opportunities.

HERE'S WHY CONTINUOUS learning is critical for solopreneurs:

Staying competitive: The pace of change in business, technology, and marketing is rapid. Solopreneurs who stay on top of industry trends, new tools, and best practices will be able to adapt quickly and stay ahead of competitors.

Embracing new technologies: Technologies like AI, blockchain, and virtual reality are transforming industries. Solopreneurs who invest time in learning about these technologies and how they can apply them to their businesses will be able to capitalize on emerging trends.

Improving personal and professional skills: From time management to digital marketing, solopreneurs need a wide range of skills to succeed. Continuous learning ensures that solopreneurs can improve their efficiency, decision-making, and overall business acumen.

By committing to lifelong learning and staying adaptable, solopreneurs can remain relevant in a rapidly changing world and continuously grow their businesses.

The future of solopreneurship is full of exciting opportunities and challenges. As trends like automation, personal branding, the gig economy, remote work, and sustainability continue to shape the business landscape, solopreneurs will need to stay agile and open to new ideas. By embracing these trends and investing in personal growth and innovation, solopreneurs can not only survive but thrive in the future.

Staying ahead of the curve means being proactive, continuously learning, and adapting to the evolving needs of your audience. By positioning yourself to take advantage of emerging trends, you can build a resilient and successful solopreneur business that grows and evolves with the times.

Why Solopreneurship is More Than a Career—It's a Lifestyle

Solopreneurship goes far beyond just being a career choice—it's a lifestyle that defines how you approach work, personal fulfillment, and the balance between the two. Unlike traditional employment, where you follow a set schedule, work for someone else's goals, and have clearly defined roles, solopreneurship offers complete autonomy over your professional life. This freedom allows you to design a business that aligns with your values, passions, and personal preferences. However, with this freedom comes responsibility and the need for discipline, resilience, and adaptability.

In this final chapter, we'll explore why solopreneurship is more than just a job or career path and how it impacts every aspect of your life. From defining your own success to blending work with personal fulfillment, solopreneurship offers a holistic lifestyle that can be incredibly rewarding if approached with the right mindset.

Freedom to Define Your Own Success

One of the most appealing aspects of solopreneurship is the ability to define success on your own terms. In a traditional job, success is often measured by external factors like promotions, salary increases, and job titles. As a solopreneur, you're in control of how you measure success, whether it's by financial gain, creative fulfillment, impact, or the lifestyle you've created.

Here's how solopreneurship allows you to define success:

Personalized goals: You get to set the goals that matter most to you. Whether your aim is to achieve financial independence, pursue a passion project, or create a business that aligns with your values, success is defined by what you want to accomplish, not by someone else's expectations.

Work-life balance: Solopreneurs have the flexibility to create a work-life balance that suits their personal needs. If success means having more time for family, travel, or hobbies, you can structure your business to support that lifestyle, without the restrictions of a 9-to-5 job.

Creative freedom: Solopreneurs have the freedom to choose the types of projects and clients they want to work with. If success means pursuing projects that ignite your creativity or passion, solopreneurship allows you to shape your business around the work you enjoy most.

By defining success on your own terms, solopreneurship becomes more than just a job—it becomes a path toward personal and professional fulfillment.

Blurring the Lines between Work and Personal Life

Solopreneurship often blurs the lines between work and personal life, but rather than seeing this as a negative, many solopreneurs embrace the fluidity. When you run your own business, your work is deeply connected to your identity and passions. As a result, solopreneurs often find that work and life blend together in a way that feels natural and fulfilling.

Here's why solopreneurship blends work and life:

Pursuing passions: Many solopreneurs build businesses around what they love. When you're passionate about your work, it no longer feels like a separate task you have to endure—it becomes something you enjoy doing, even during your personal time. This creates a seamless blend between work and life, where both aspects feed into each other.

Flexibility and autonomy: Solopreneurs have the freedom to choose when and where they work. Whether you prefer to work from home, a coffee shop, or while traveling, solopreneurship offers the flexibility to structure your work around your life, not the other way around. You can attend to personal commitments or take breaks when needed, making it easier to integrate your business with your lifestyle.

Personal growth: As a solopreneur, your business challenges are often personal challenges. Running a business requires constant learning, resilience, and self-improvement, which contributes to your personal growth. The lessons you learn in business—whether it's about problem-solving, time management, or self-discipline—also benefits your personal life.

Solopreneurship can be incredibly fulfilling because it allows you to build a life that's fully integrated with your work, giving you the freedom to live authentically.

Building a Business That Reflects your Values

Solopreneurs have the unique opportunity to build businesses that reflect their personal values and beliefs. Whether it's creating a sustainable product, promoting social good, or fostering community, solopreneurs can design their businesses to have a positive impact on the world in ways that matter to them.

Here's how solopreneurship aligns with your values:

Purpose-driven work: Many solopreneurs choose to build businesses that are aligned with their personal values or a mission they care about. For example, you might start a business that promotes eco-friendly practices, supports underserved communities, or advocates for social change. When your business reflects your values, your work becomes more meaningful and fulfilling.

AUTHENTIC BRANDING: Solopreneurs often create brands that are deeply personal and authentic. This allows you to connect with your audience on a deeper level, as your business represents not just a product or service, but also the values and beliefs you stand for. Authenticity can build trust and loyalty, making your brand stand out in a crowded market.

Conscious decision-making: Solopreneurs have full control over their business decisions, which means you can choose partners, suppliers, and clients who align with your values. You're not forced to compromise your beliefs for the sake of profit, and you can make conscious choices that reflect the impact you want your business to have.

By building a business that reflects your values, solopreneurship offers the chance to create something that's not only profitable but also purpose-driven and aligned with your personal beliefs.

The Challenge of Self-Discipline and Accountability

While solopreneurship offers freedom and flexibility, it also comes with the responsibility of self-discipline and accountability. Without a boss or team to oversee your work, you're entirely responsible for managing your time, staying productive, and ensuring your business thrives. This can be both empowering and challenging.

Here's how solopreneurship fosters self-discipline and accountability:

Setting your own schedule: The freedom to set your own hours is one of the perks of solopreneurship, but it requires strong time management skills. Without structure, it's easy to procrastinate or lose focus. Solopreneurs must develop the discipline to create and stick to a schedule that keeps them productive and on track.

Staying accountable: When you're your own boss, there's no one to hold you accountable but yourself. This requires a high level of responsibility and a strong sense of accountability. Setting clear goals, tracking your progress, and staying committed to your business vision are essential for success as a solopreneur.

Learning to say no: Solopreneurs have the freedom to choose which projects or clients to work with, but that also means learning to say no to opportunities that don't align with your goals or values. This requires discipline, as it can be tempting to take on every opportunity, even if it's not the right fit for your business.

Solopreneurship teaches valuable lessons in self-discipline, time management, and accountability, which are essential skills for both business and personal success.

CONTINUOUS LEARNING and Adaptation

Solopreneurship is a journey of continuous learning and adaptation. As the business world evolves, so must solopreneurs. This requires staying open to new ideas, learning new skills, and being adaptable in the face of change. The willingness to grow, both personally and professionally, is what allows solopreneurs to thrive in the long term.

Here's how solopreneurship fosters continuous learning:

Staying relevant: In an ever-changing market, solopreneurs must stay up-to-date with industry trends, technological advancements, and consumer behavior. Continuous learning ensures that you stay relevant and competitive in your field, whether it's through online courses, workshops, or staying informed through industry publications.

Embracing failure as a learning opportunity: Solopreneurs often face setbacks and failures, but these challenges provide valuable lessons. By embracing failure as part of the learning process, solopreneurs can adapt, refine their strategies, and ultimately grow stronger from the experience.

Personal and professional growth: Solopreneurship challenges you to step outside your comfort zone, take risks, and learn new skills. Whether it's mastering marketing, improving communication, or developing leadership abilities, solopreneurs must be willing to invest in their own growth to succeed.

By adopting a mindset of continuous learning, solopreneurs can adapt to new challenges, innovate, and stay ahead of the curve in their industry.

Crafting a Life of Fulfillment and Purpose

At its core, solopreneurship is about crafting a life of fulfillment and purpose. It's the freedom to pursue your passions, create something meaningful, and design a lifestyle that aligns with your values. Solopreneurship offers the unique opportunity to integrate work with personal fulfillment, making it more than just a career—it's a way of life.

Here's how solopreneurship leads to a fulfilling lifestyle:

Pursuing what you love: Solopreneurs often build businesses around their passions and interests, which leads to a more fulfilling and enjoyable work experience. When you're doing what you love, work feels less like a chore and more like a creative expression of who you are.

Making an impact: Many solopreneurs are driven by the desire to make a positive impact, whether it's through their products, services, or contributions to their community. This sense of purpose adds meaning to their work and creates a deeper connection to their business.

Living life on your terms: Solopreneurship gives you the freedom to design your life in a way that aligns with your values and aspirations. Whether it's achieving financial independence, having the flexibility to travel, or spending more time with family, solopreneurs have the autonomy to create a life that reflects their true desires. By blending work, passion, and purpose, solopreneurship allows you to create a life that's not only successful but also deeply fulfilling.

Solopreneurship is far more than just a career—it's a lifestyle that offers the freedom, flexibility, and fulfillment that many people seek in their professional and personal lives. From defining your own success to building a business that reflects your values, solopreneurship gives you the autonomy to create a life that's uniquely yours. However, with this freedom comes responsibility. Solopreneurs must cultivate self-discipline, accountability, and a mindset of continuous learning to thrive in an ever-changing business landscape. By embracing the challenges and opportunities that solopreneurship presents, you can craft a lifestyle that's rich with purpose, passion, and personal fulfillment. Ultimately, solopreneurship is about more than just making a living—it's about designing a life that aligns with your values, passions, and goals, allowing you to live authentically and achieve true success on your own terms.